Emptiness an

GW01424389

Du Zhijun

Cam River Publishing

First English Edition Published in Great Britain

By CAM RIVERS PUBLISHING LTD 2022
33 Trumpington Street
Cambridge CB2 1QY

DU Zhijun

Emptiness and Wisdom

Translator: Jack Hargreaves
Editor: Emma Nortfors
Project manager: QIN Yuchen, LI Yue
Book Design: QIN Yubin (MUYE)
Cover Design: GE Dalong
Illustrator: DU Li

A CIP Catalogue of this book is available
from the British Library

ISBN: 978-1-912603-68-8

press@cambridgerivers.com
www.cambridgerivers.com

Contents

INTRODUCTION

Life is marred by sundry afflictions. Birth, ageing, sickness, and death; union and parting, loss and gain, setbacks and frustrations; worries, despondence, and disputes—they plague and hinder us every moment of every day. With this book the author hopes, by shedding light on the great mystery of Buddhist emptiness, to guide readers onto the path to liberation.

Buddhist Dharma tells us that all suffering and vexation arises from our own mind, and that if we desire liberation from them, we must start by purifying ourselves. The human mind possesses a dual nature, it contains a self aspect and a non-self aspect. The former, the self-nature of mind, is nothing more than an amalgamation of causal conditions, it does not truly exist; the latter, the non-self nature of mind—our Buddha nature—is what truly requires our attention, our illumination, because to rediscover that is the way to escape suffering once and for all.

Look to nature—to the skies and the earth, to water and fire, to the sunlight and air—for the wisdom of emptiness. Allow the universal laws of nature to guide your understanding of Buddhist Dharma and your cultivation of its teachings. And just maybe, you will find your own path to freedom from life's suffering.

CHAPTER ONE

Dependent Origination

All origination is dependent. Everything results from the coming together of causes and conditions. The circumstances for me to begin my journey with Buddhist Dharma aligned when I read the Diamond Sutra.

My journey with Buddhist Dharma started with reading the Diamond Sutra. It was in 2013 that I picked the volume out at random from the bookshelf. Only a few pages in, the scripture had me under its spell. 'The Dharma, infinitely profound and subtle, is rarely encountered even in a million aeons.' The vivid metaphors, the richly philosophical language – they drew me to the Dharma they described. To gain a better understanding of what I was reading, I bought every book on the market that provided an explanation of the text. In them, I came across terms like the 'True Principle', 'Wisdom' and 'Non-self', and phrases about 'calming the mind' and 'bringing an end to suffering'. They were each part of the common language of Buddhist Dharma and they triggered something in me that, once started, I could not stop. I could work out the meaning of some of them, like 'everything is as illusory as a dream or a bubble'; 'nothing is permanent'; 'all emotion is suffering'. Others only created more questions: 'everything is empty'; 'all phenomena are void of self'; 'the realisation of Nirvana'. I read dozens of Buddhist texts and books on Buddhism, once, twice, three times over, and gradually I formed a clearer idea of what many Dharmic concepts mean, and what Dharma itself is. But the notions of an essential emptiness, of non-self and of Nirvana still eluded me. Nonetheless, with the instruction of the Diamond Sutra, I had begun a Buddhist practice. Had my friend never gifted me that book, the rest of the causes and conditions that had led me to this point might never have fallen into place, and I wouldn't have the practice I do today, nor would I be writing this.

Still, I made no ground when it came to those core concepts of Emptiness and Nirvana. A friend took me to an event at a temple, and I started attending meetings at other temples myself in an attempt to benefit from a more varied approach to my studies. I gradually gained a greater awareness of my personal experiences with attachment, self-centredness and karma. I came to know, at an intellectual level, that 'ignorance' is our worst enemy and the source of all our suffering. But, thinking back now, I realise that in every one of those meetings the attendees repeatedly referred to 'ignorance' and 'attachment', whereas I rarely heard anyone mention 'emptiness' or 'non-self'.

While I remained unable to solve these puzzles, my Dharmic practice seemed only to progress so far. Practitioner friends shared their own methods with me, which I put to use, but each only partially solved the problem. Many of my emotional issues required addressing at their root, but I was still too confused about certain elements of the teachings of Dharma to glean from them the lessons they provide. My life lacked direction and was marred by suffering.

My regular discussion group organised a trip to stay at a monastery for a few days to get a taste of temple life. As I sat drinking tea and talking with one of the masters, I took the chance to ask him what is meant within the Dharma by wisdom. 'Master, I've heard that Wisdom and Emptiness are advanced concepts to try and understand. Could you take a moment to explain them to me, please?' His answer was not what I had hoped. He very tactfully sidestepped the question and led the conversation onto another topic while continuing to sip his tea. The conversation I had so been looking forward to ended shortly after. Afterward, I realised what I should have taken away from this was that my foundation in Dharmic learning needed more work. I had to practice and experience the lessons of Dharma for much longer, and cultivate greater merit, before the chance for me to grasp Emptiness would present itself. I went home, crestfallen, and immediately threw myself into my daily practice, newly rejuvenated in my determination to study Emptiness.

At some point, I bought the book *Old Path White Clouds: Walking in the Footsteps of the Buddha*, written by Zen Master Thich Nhat Hanh. Reading it grabbed me in the same way the *Diamond Sutra* had. I read it over and over and applied what I learned to my daily life. Then I re-read it some more. I studied its teachings and searched for their truth around me. After having read it through no less than fifty times, finally the day came when it all seemed to click.

Old Path White Clouds is widely considered the most influential record of the Buddha's life and teachings. It traces the events some 2,600 years ago of the Buddha growing up, renouncing mundane society, cultivating the Way and reaching enlightenment, and pairs them with the oral teachings he imparted to others while he was still alive. These are the original Dharma. With every line of his instruction that I read, I felt as if the Buddha was at my side, present and real. I sensed my practice was on the right path. I realised that the Dharma is based in the essence of the universe and all things. In the Dharma, the Buddha gave us his explanation of the true principle of the universe.

The true or universal principle, Emptiness, the essential nature of things, substantiality, reality, the true form – these words appear more than most in the Dharma and all share a similar meaning. Buddhist teachers often use them interchangeably as the situation or recipient of their instruction requires. The Buddha once said, 'The only way to become free of ignorance is by seeing all things for what they truly are, by perceiving their true nature; ignorance is the source of all suffering.' Here, when the Buddha talks of 'perceiving their true nature', he is referring to the essence of all things, their essential Emptiness. A Buddhist elder once said, 'Buddhism is only interested in one thing, that is to realise the truth, the true principle of all things; ridding oneself of desires is not the ultimate goal of Buddhism. Rather, its goal is to realise the universal principle.' Here, the notions of perceiving the true nature of things and of realising the truth mean much the same. To Buddhist practitioners, both are paramount to cultivating a successful practice.

So, what is the true principle? And what is the relationship between the true principle and wisdom? For anyone who loves Buddhist philosophy, gaining clarity about these concepts – truth and wisdom – is a helpful step toward understanding and even practising its teachings.

What, then, is the true principle? If an idea or characteristic describes the essence of the universe, if it reflects the essence of all things, if it can exist and change independently of anything else, if it is invariably correct or true under any circumstance at any time, then, that it is a true principle. What's more, any view of things established on the basis of this principle is an understanding based in truth, and an understanding based in truth is the only one sturdy enough to support wisdom. That means it takes a person transcending normal modes of thought and gaining insight into the essence of all phenomena in the world, and universe, for us to reasonably be able to call them wise. Buddhist Dharma prioritises truth and wisdom. It guides us through truth and wisdom towards correcting our thinking and habits and cleansing our minds. These are the necessary steps Dharma teaches we must take before we can rid ourselves of afflictions, free ourselves from suffering, and purify ourselves of ego, thereby attaining the goal of manifesting our Buddha nature.

And the essential nature of all things? Emptiness? The core of Buddhist Dharma? What are they, and how can they help us cleanse our minds? How can we use them to stop our suffering? These questions are central to grasping Buddhist Dharma and cultivating a productive practice of its teachings. They are worth spending a whole life studying and exploring.

The Dharma is concerned with the essential quality of phenomena beneath their external appearances. What it can show us of the world and everything in it derives from superhuman insight. If we lack for life experience, or, in other words, if we lack karmic merit, truly understanding Buddhist Dharma is a nearly impossible task.. There are thousands of Buddhist texts full of Dharmic sayings and theories, each with a strong logic that is often laid out in arcane language and abstract anecdotes. So to read, not to mention understand, their content is not an easy task. It is first requires us to wrap our heads around the Dharma's two distinct methods of discussing the universe: in relative terms and in absolute terms. The former refer to the conditional and to the conditionality of things, to the fact that everything relies on dependent origination for its existence. This description of things, in particular, is intended as a convenient linguistic tool to facilitate our understanding of the world around us, what is what is definite, unconditional, unchanging, eternal or independent. Birth, death, beginnings and endings, for example, are all relative terms. Their origination or occurrence or existence depend on what Buddhism refers to as causes and conditions – essentially, any factor that contributes to one thing the origination of something else.

Absoluteness, on the other hand, describes the continuous flux of the myriad things of the universe. All things have evolved, one manifestation or stage at a time, from a single material source at the beginning of the cosmos. That material source developed, in turn, from whatever substance preceded the universe. So, it is impossible to deduce the beginnings of things and equally impossible to predict their end. In absolute terms, things have no beginning and no end, and nor does their 'source'.

Anyone who reads this book cover to cover will learn that the intrinsic, essential nature of all things is Emptiness. They will know this nature is eternally unchanging, constant, and that Emptiness is also eternally unchanging and constant. It is absolute. Finishing this book will give you a clear notion of what is relative and what is absolute.

To make understanding Buddhist Dharma easier for everyone, to help you grasp the core of Dharma as well as its wisdom, in this book I will introduce the essential nature of all things, Dharmic Emptiness, from my own perspective. We will first explore these concepts through the lens of how the universe came to be and how it continues to unfold, before turning our attention to more quotidian aspects of life and how Dharma relates to them, in the hope that, by taking this approach, you might find you make some unexpected leaps in your learning along the way. There is no harm in trying anyway.

Before we start, it's important to note that phrases like 'the essence of the myriad things and events in the universe' and 'the essential nature of phenomena' feature repeatedly. But what we mean by them is fundamentally the same. Things, events, phenomena, only have a slightly different emphasis which might benefit certain situations or people. But for our purposes, and in this book, there is no clear difference between them.

Every one of us is an individual with unique perspectives and experiences. But origination is invariably dependent. Everything arises from the coming together of causes and conditions, so whether or not after reading this book you identify with its content, whether or not you accept it, it is all a matter of your, the reader's, causes and conditions of your perspective. If this book can bring readers to the same frequency as me, I am sure we will be like old friends reunited, and what a feeling of indescribable gratitude and joy that would be.

I wish for your circumstances – your causes and conditions – to align, so you can foster a comprehensive understanding of the ultimate truth; I wish for your practice and realisations to bring you to Buddhahood; I wish for you to achieve true liberation from affliction and suffering.

CHAPTER TWO

The Essence of the Myriad Things, the Root of Dharma

The myriad things of the universe depend on the alignment of causes and conditions for their origination. Their appearance is inconstant. Their essence is Emptiness. This is the universal principle the Buddha discovered about the true nature of the cosmos; it is also a core tenet of Buddhist Dharma. Dharma's prajna[1] wisdom and wisdom of emptiness both derive from cognition of the essential nature of the myriad things.

It is difficult to understand just how large the universe is. It is a distance scientists measure using the speed of light, the fastest thing in the universe as far as we know. At 300,000 kilometres per second, light travels from the sun to Earth's surface in a matter of eight minutes and eighteen seconds. In the space of a year, it covers around 9.4607×1012 kilometres. That's nine trillion, four hundred and sixty billion, seven hundred million kilometres; or 9,460,700,000,000 km. That's one lightyear, quite the distance already, so scientists calculate the distances between celestial bodies within a galaxy using single digit lightyears. Yet present astronomical research shows that the Milky Way, within which our solar system lies, is larger than ten lightyears across, and the diameter of the universe far surpasses what we can humanly imagine. Some scientists even believe it could be boundless. Cosmologists have managed to estimate the distance between certain planets as at least ten billion lightyears.

What's more, within that universe there could be around a trillion other planets like Earth. Compared with the vast, far-reaching universe that contains it, the planet we call home seems minute and insignificant, not to mention the tiny humans who who inhabit it. Finding the underlying truth of the universe, then,

---

[1] **Prajñā** or **paññā**, is a Buddhist term often translated as "wisdom", "intelligence", or "understanding". It is described in Buddhist commentaries as the understanding of the true nature of phenomena.

the cosmic law of nature which ties everything together, is surely easier said than done?

This is especially true as it is our habit to view things and events at only the surface level. Only with a concerted effort can we penetrate deeper, beyond the superficial, and rarely beyond that to the intrinsic essence of a thing. On the outside, the world around us appears diverse and ever-changing. But if we never observe beyond that aspect of things, we will never see to the principle guiding the origination of all things, to the true form beneath their appearance. What we see is only the surface and not the true form of anything.

The Buddha was an exceptional figure. His greatness derived from his ability to perceive the world from a heightened perspective and see clear through the many layers of haze that hide the true state of things. Around 2,600 years ago, before humankind had any of the understanding of the cosmos, space, and Earth we have today, the Buddha managed to uncover the essential nature of life and the universe. He saw the formation, flourishing, deterioration and end of countless worlds unfold, he perceived the myriad things of the cosmos contained within every cell of his body, he saw how everything is conditional, he felt how

No phenomenon is borne of a single element. Every phenomenon is dependent on other phenomena for its origination, development and disintegration. Soil, water, a seed, a tree, the sun, the passage of time, space – these are all necessary elements for the growth of a leaf. Remove just one of them and the leaf cannot grow. ▶▶

all existence is interdependent. His discovery revealed to him the interconnectedness of the world around him. It showed him how no phenomenon is borne of a single element. Every phenomenon is dependent on other phenomena for its origination, development and disintegration. Soil, water, a seed, a tree, the sun, the passage of time, space – these are all necessary elements for the growth of a leaf. Remove just one of them and the leaf cannot grow.

The Buddha saw right back to the beginnings of humankind and beyond, to the formation of the universe. *Old Path White Clouds* quotes the Buddha as saying that before he was a human, he had lived many lives as soil, stone, plants, birds and other animals. His existence originated from long before any of these even existed on Earth, as do all of ours, but he was able to tune in to the true nature of the universe, Earth, and all worldly things. Such insights transcend time. Even today, more than two thousand years later, the Buddha's perception of things is still revered by many as the truth.

Recognising this truth, this universal principle, is a vital step to manifesting wisdom. The universal principle is independent and unchanging; it remains, under any circumstance and in every situation, absolutely and eternally true. It is a direct reflection of the essence of the universe and all phenomena. As he sat under the bodhi tree, the Buddha realised that the origination of every phenomenon depends on the coming together of two or more elements. In Dharma, these elements or factors are known as causes and conditions. This truth about the myriad things is in and of itself one of the only things that is not established or conditional. It simply identifies an essential quality within all phenomena. Even one hundred million years from now, it will remain correct. The Buddha based his Dharma on this universal principle; on an understanding of the essential nature of the universe and the myriad things it contains.

Our individual perspectives, often ego-driven and limited, can only see a part of the whole, whereas a 'non-self perspective', based in non-self, or selflessness, and in alignment with the collective, can perceive the whole picture. The former allows a breadth of experience like that of a frog in a well; the latter promises an expansive, more comprehensive outlook – it is what is described in the Dharma as the true view of things, based in wisdom and in an understanding of the universal principle. Wisdom is a rare thing to have and can change the course of our life. If we have it, we can live wisely.

Perspectives are not something we lack for. Every business, every field, every affair, they all have their outlooks, just as each one of us does, and we change them or acquire new ones after almost everything that happens. But if we really pay attention, we notice that the one constant across all these perspectives is the primacy of 'I', of the self. Our mundane perspectives mostly derive from our experiences, which themselves stem from certain causes and conditions, which we judge using a differentiating, dualist mindset, meaning, for instance, that we invariably evaluate our experiences as either good or bad. It is our habit either to divide the whole into parts or to view a part as the whole picture, so of course our perspectives are limited. But while things are going in our favour, we believe our perspective to be right – until our luck changes. Then our perspective appears flawed. Clearly, there is a lot to be desired when it comes to the mundane, worldly way of looking at and approaching the world. This is why Dharma places so much emphasis on perspective. Buddhism teaches us that our perspective dictates our world view and values, which lead to the motivations we identify with and the actions we take. Our intent and behaviour are what accumulate our karma, determine our fortune and the kind of life we have.

Origination is dependent on causes and conditions – this is the universal principle. It is an essential quality of the cosmos and the myriad things that have arisen and continue to arise dependent on other phenomena. Dharma, as created by the Buddha, is founded on this tenet. Therein lies its most profound insight and its wisdom.

At this point, you might be thinking about asking, what good, if any, does recognising the essential nature of things do for us? Well, let's think about it for a moment, and you might be surprised to find just how significant the changes are that it can make in our lives. For one, seeing to essence of things relieves us of having to ask ourselves the question, What is the truth? Phenomena – events and things – are ever-shifting and take on different appearances in every context. They can be better than we ever imagined or worse than we can handle, and more often than not we do not know which they'll be. If these manifestations, that we cannot help but attach value judgements to, are all we can perceive, we are doomed to live in constant anxiety, fear, annoyance, pain, confusion and ignorance, as our expectations lead us by the nose through every experience. Also, the myriad things, which depend on causes and conditions for their origination, and which change and shift along with the arrangements of elements that make them up in the same way humans do, never experience a shred of suffering, unlike humans. Why is this? At the core of it is the fact that the myriad things are aligned with their nature of non-self – their lack of any inherent self. Devoid of any notion of self, they do not differentiate; since they do not differentiate, they do not develop attachments; free of attachments, they do not suffer. Such is the value of no self-nature.

The thing is, humans themselves constitute a group within the myriad things, and we too possess an essential non-self. In us, it manifests as a non-self attitude. It is inherent to us like it is to every phenomenon, only the essential nature of non-self within us is also known as Buddha-nature. The reason we might be oblivious to this aspect of ourselves, why it may never have manifested in our being, is that the self-nature of mind – the ego – obscures it. It is therefore our mission first to recognise this essential nature of non-self in all the myriad things, then to recognise it in ourselves and take steps to realign with that intrinsic aspect of our being, the natural state of non-self. If we achieve this, our afflictions and suffering will vanish.

Buddhist Dharma is tied to the true principle. It is based on that universal truth the Buddha awoke to, which penetrates past the superficial appearance of things to their essential nature. It is rare to be able to understand this principle easily. For this reason, in an effort to make the profound truth of the universe more accessible, the Buddha invented eighty-four thousand methods of study, all of which lead to the same realisations, but in their diversity offer a wide variety of paths. The Buddha hoped this would provide everyone with an approach to studying the Dharma that suits them and thereby help as many people as possible toward alleviating the suffering and afflictions in their lives. I remember one story that recounts the time the Buddha, worried people would fail to grasp this great truth through having it taught them alone, chose to abandon his mission and remain in the forest where he could live in peace, unconcerned by the suffering elsewhere in the world. The tale goes that the gods Śakra and Brahmā caught wind of what the Buddha was thinking and manifested before him to implore the Buddha not to hide himself in the forest. They persuaded him that while not everybody would understand, the benefit he would provide to the few that did understand the lessons made sharing his wisdom worthwhile. The Buddha obeyed their request and left the forest to begin teaching about the path to liberation.

From here, let us follow in the footsteps of scientists before us and explore the origin of the universe and the myriad things, the quiddity of those myriad things and the universal principle which underlies their existence.

Where did the universe come from? Where did the myriad things come from? What is the essential nature of the myriad things? These are philosophical questions as well as scientific ones. To answer them, and not only answer them but to align our cognition with the truths they reveal, is the key to unlocking our wisdom.

In terms of time, the universe came first. In terms of space, the universe is the largest; it contains everything else. So, for the most fundamental view of the myriad things, we should start by discussing the origin of the universe.

How the universe came about, or in other words, how it began, is a mystery. At present, scientists believe it expanded out of a vast explosion, called the Big Bang, 13.8 billion years ago. Specifically, it came into being out of a singularity, a single point of infinite mass, infinite pressure and infinitely high temperatures, where time and space were infinitely distorted. This originary material, which scientists believe contained the whole of the universe as we know it, exploded and rapidly expanded, at first chaotically, then over time in an ever more orderly way, until the mass, lightyears across, began to rotate and form a disk-shaped system in constant motion. Within this system, there was a constant process of fusion and transformation taking place, which eventually produced galaxies, and within our galaxy, the solar system, and within the solar system, the eight planets, one of which was the Earth, the only one now still able to support life. A hundred million years ago, dinosaurs dominated the food chain on Earth. After dinosaurs went extinct, humans emerged, and we rose to become the apex being predator on Earth, where we are the most advanced form of intelligence.

The 'universe' is an astronomical term created by humans. Strictly speaking, before the Big Bang there was no universe as such, only the singularity. One thing we know for certain about that material is that it was not singular in its composition. Single, independent elements are still, immutable, constant and eternal. The singularity was none of those things. As the Big Bang confirms, it was made up of countless elements, just as its formation, the Big Bang, and the beginnings of Earth and all the other planets were processes helped along by countless factors. To this day, no one knows what the universe was like before the Big Bang. No one knows what anything was like before the Big Bang. But we do know that the explosion of some supermassive material set in motion the trajectory of the universe.

Clearly, the power causes and conditions have over the universe and its contents is immeasurable. They have pushed along its formation and evolution from the existence of the singularity to the present moment. Although there remains much we do not

14

know about the Big Bang and the universe around that time, there are a few things we know to be true, one of which is the timeless discovery made by the Buddha when he attained enlightenment, that 'Origination is dependent. The universe and the myriad things result from the coming together of causes and conditions,' such is the origin of cosmos and everything we know. This truth describes the essential nature of the myriad things and underlies the workings of the universe.

Nothing appears or happens without cause. Nothing emerges from thin air or out of nothingness. The Milky Way and solar system, every material, every event, every phenomenon, all depend on the causes and conditions of their origination, and how they change, move and evolve is driven by transformations and shifts in the many factors contributing to their being. Causes and conditions must exist for their mutual harmony to produce phenomena. Without them, there is no universe, no myriad things, no humankind.

What, then, do these things, material and phenomenal, have of their own? What belongs to them? What is their essence? Conceptually, essence refers to something's innate internal quality and characteristics. It determines what qualities and characteristics that thing has; determines its nature. Essence, therefore, signifies nature; essence is nature. Fortunately, for our purposes, essence, nature, and essential nature all share a similar meaning.

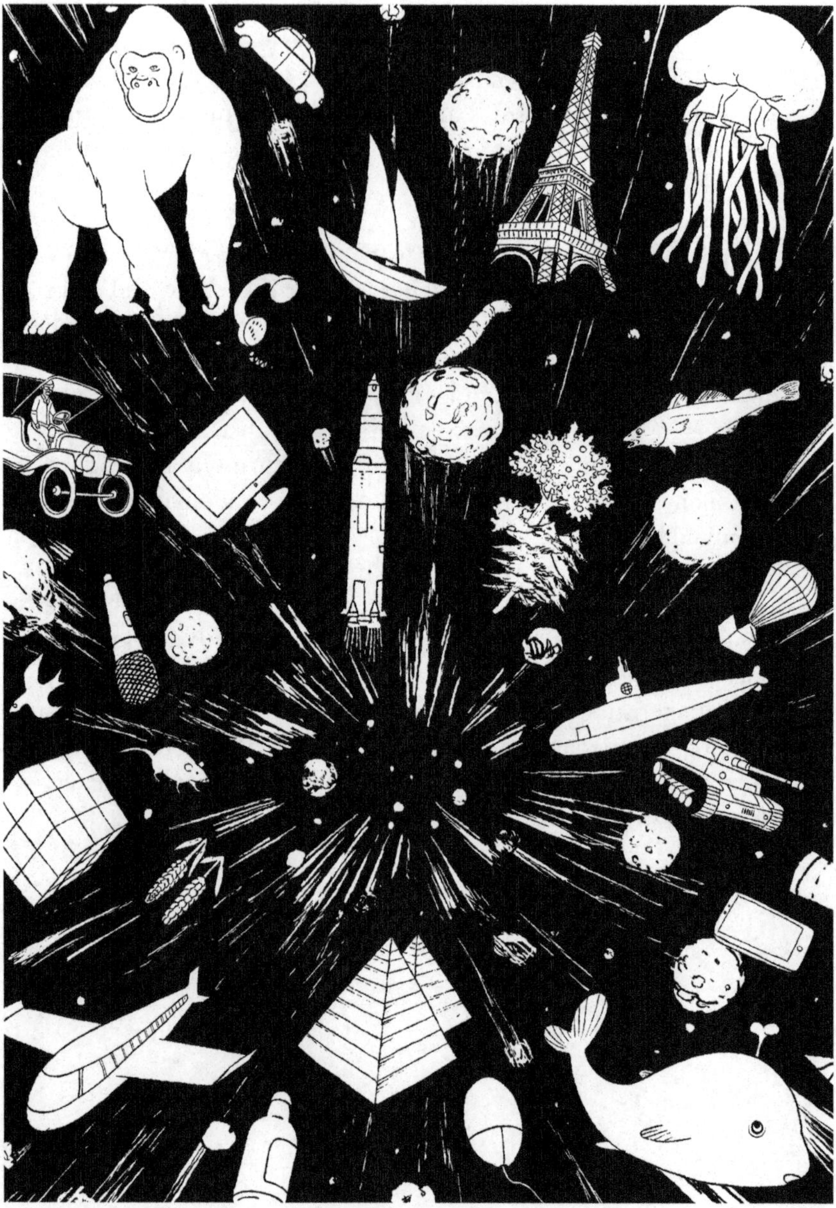

Everything results from the harmony of causes and conditions, the power of which is hard to grasp. Causes and conditions are behind the evolution of the cosmos and its contents, stage by stage, from its originary material to its present form. ◄◄

Since the myriad things of the universe derive from the harmony of causes and conditions, they possess no inherent, essential self. Instead, they have an internal, essential nature of 'non-self'. In addition to 'non-self', because their external manifestations exist in continuous flux due to the dependence of their make-up on external factors, 'impermanence' is another characteristic of their internal, essential nature. Impermanence and non-self comprise the essential nature of the cosmos. They are the real, constant, unchanging characteristics the universal principle reveals to us, and if we can tune into them, they are effective tools for dispelling our deluded, incorrect view of things.

The essence of a thing determines its nature. The myriad things thus have the quality of Emptiness. Void of any inherent self, they possess no eternal, immutable, individual quality. Not even the source of the universe, before its origination with the Big Bang, had an independent, unchanging, perpetual existence. The most fundamental characteristic of the myriad things is non-self; non-self is the essential nature of all phenomena. The Buddha taught that non-self is the noumenon of the myriad things, the one independent, consistent existence there is. It remains universal, now and always. No one thing is inherently imbued with self; each thing is the result of the harmony of causes and conditions. When a change occurs in the cause and conditions that make up a phenomenon, it engenders a change in the manifestation, whether material or phenomenal, of that phenomenon. This is a continuous, ever-shifting process of the combination, abiding and separation of causes and conditions. It is what dictates the birth, aging, sickness and death of sentient beings and the completion, abiding, devolution and absence of other phenomena. Everything in the mundane world exists in constant flux; nothing exists in stasis, stillness or perpetual unchanging.

Here, I need to make it clear that while the myriad things all possess an essential nature, this essential nature and the myriad things are not one and the same thing. The essential nature of the myriad things is unaffected by changes in causes and conditions. It is absolute, immutable, permanent. It never increases or decreases, comes into being or ceases to exist. Whereas the myriad things are all of those things and undergo all of those changes. They depend on the causes and conditions of their origination and change in accordance with these causes and conditions. Each of their various manifestations is impermanent – it is as if they were illusory.

This is why Buddhist Dharma is focussed on the essential 'impermanence' and 'non-self' at the core of all phenomena, while it is the habit of us laypeople to concentrate on the external, ostensible 'permanence' and 'self' of phenomena, even to the degree of attachment. We are used to viewing surface manifestations as real, as actual existences. The quotidian, mundane conception of 'existence' and Dharma's conception of it, however, could not be more different. For the worldly, existence is what we can perceive; it is what is substantial; it is 'presence'. Dharma has its own standards by which to judge 'existence'.

Buddhist Dharma identifies existence, and that which exists, as being independent of causes and conditions. Existence signifies permanence and immutability. Any result of causes and conditions does not truly exist; it can at best be said to be manifest. Like a flash in the pan; or like the udambara, which blooms for a matter of hours each year before its flowers wilt – any product of causes and conditions manifests for only the briefest moment in the scope of all of existence. Except we insist on their existence; we grow attached to the flower's stunning beauty, blind to its essential emptiness. Dharma, though, teaches us to see that emptiness, to regard these phenomena as fleeting manifestations, devoid of existence. And what goes for the udambara also goes for a mountain, and for all phenomena, regardless of whether they manifest for a day or ten thousand years. They depend on causes and conditions for their origination, abiding, transformation, devolution and disappearance. The mountains and rivers of this world are all slowly changing and will ultimately disappear. Surely, it is better to say that they are 'manifest' than that they 'exist'.

If we think about our experience for a moment, it quickly

becomes clear that everything we perceive to exist, be it material or phenomenal, is really only a transient and partial manifestation. In fact, there is no such thing as a complete, constant manifestation, since every phenomenon is composed of multiple stages, and a phenomenon never manifests in its entirety in an instantaneous manner. What we perceive as material things and events happening around us are simply products of our own invention.

The Buddha's goal in designing Buddhist Dharma was to help sentient beings cure themselves of life's suffering and afflictions. Ridding oneself of life's suffering and afflictions requires freeing oneself of all attachments to the myriad things. So the Buddha had to find a way of teaching why we should not develop attachments to the myriad things and why attachments are dangerous in the first place. To do this, he showed the myriad things to be like dreams – illusory. *The Diamond Sutra* contains the teaching, 'All conditioned phenomena are like a dream, an illusion, a bubble, a shadow, like the dew, or like lightning, you should discern them like this[2].' This is something we already intuitively know. It's sometimes how we speak about those moments or events that seem to pass quickly, too fast for us to even take them in, so that they feel like a dream. If we pay careful attention to this sensation, we notice in the coming and going of these moments and phenomena that their manifestation depends on causes and conditions, as do their passing.

Think about it, everything we think we possess, whether it be a material object or a characteristic we identify with, came to us through a series of events – through a series of conditions aligning – and disappeared when those factors ceased to be in place. Gain and loss are controlled by factors we cannot predict. Life experience tells us that there is no way to grasp how much time passes between a phenomenon manifesting and disappearing.

2
    A. Charles Muller, trans. The Diamond Sutra, ch. 32, http://www.acmuller.net/bud-canon/diamond_sutra. html (accessed May 27, 2021)

Whether it endures a long time, or no more than an instant, the phenomenon itself and the period of its manifestation are both invariably changeable and inconstant. This is especially true of certain phenomena which vanish almost as soon as they appear, like a flash of lightning. How changeable the phenomena of the world are often exceeds our expectations, so it is best to keep in mind that they are 'illusory'. This is a helpful tool for weakening our attachment to them and in turn reducing our afflictions and suffering.

Yet, phenomena, though illusory, are not 'non-existent', and nor are they mere illusion. Phenomena are simply like a dream; they are like illusions. The Buddha taught that 'phenomena are not non-existent.'

Ordinary society has its own standards for what is 'non-existent'. Some schools of thought consider subjects they are unsure how to talk about to be 'non-existent', others what they cannot see with their eyes, and others still what is illusory or appears and disappears without explanation. One obvious example of this debate comes from the question, is death our absolute end? Of course, Buddhist Dharma does not approve of these notions of 'non-existence'. It is not wrong in this viewpoint. Consider how frighteningly massive the universe is. Astronomers and scientists estimate it contains around one trillion planets similar to Earth and the furthest distance between any two planets is ten billion lightyears. Humanity is a mere speck of dust in the cosmos. The universe has been unfolding and expanding now for 13.8 billion years. The time humans have spent on Earth is but a blip in that timeline, and the several thousand years of our recorded civilised history is even tinier. Indeed, it isn't hard to question how much humanity really knows about the universe. So how can we lump together all those things we cannot easily see or understand as 'non-existent'?

In the Dharmic conception of things, not only does everything not 'exist', but it simultaneously does not 'not-exist'. It neither occupies a state of 'existence', nor 'non-existence'. It endures in a state between the two. Dharma calls this in-between state 'manifestation,' and it is a state of limitless possibilities and variation.

According to the Dharmic definition of 'existence', besides the essential nature of the myriad things, nothing else in the mundane realm can be said to exist. Everything else is nothing more than a manifestation. Manifestations have no fixed state, they can appear one way one moment and another way the next. They take many forms and are illusory.

Dharma explains that these manifestations arise from the harmony of unstable and impermanent causes and conditions, which are always changing and shifting, and which in turn put these manifestations in a constant state of flux. Some changes occur quickly, some visibly and some overtly, in a way everyone can see with the naked eye; others occur slowly, secretly, subtly, imperceptibly.

Scientists have proven that change is constant. There is no moment when it is not occurring, whether we perceive it or not. That phenomena are in a constant state of change is an indisputable fact. A helpful metaphor for understanding this is that of a river. When we look at a river one moment, turn away, then look back, there doesn't appear to be any difference, but we know the river is in flow and there are things happening beneath its surface or upstream or downstream from where we are that we cannot perceive. The river is constantly changing in accordance with its causes and conditions. Just because we cannot see it, does not mean it is not true. Another analogy is that of the sun, which explodes and burns at every moment, transforming throughout each millisecond of every second, yet the sun we see today and the sun we saw yesterday appear much the same to us, even to the extent that special instruments might not identify any differences. So, change is not always something we can easily observe.

On Earth, there is no change more subtle than the planet's rotation. Since human records began, several thousand years ago,

Earth has spun on its axis at a mostly steady speed of around twenty-three hours, fifty-six minutes and four seconds per rotation, and it has never faltered. It is believed, however, that early on in the Earth's existence, a single rotation only took around six hours and that it has gradually slowed since then. Fast-forward to several billion years ago, a single cycle lasted eighteen hours. So, it is clear that by calculating the speed of the Earth's rotation using seconds as the unit of measurement, the speed would appear constant. If we were to measure it using microseconds, the change would be evident.

Even now, the universe continues to expand, and the moon is gradually moving away from Earth. The time it takes for Earth to rotate once increases by more than a dozen microseconds every day. Eventually, after another several hundred million years, perhaps one Earth day will last twenty-five hours, or even longer. Whether or not humankind will be around to record that historical change we cannot know. Everything is in a state of flux. When few changes take place in the causes and conditions of a manifestation, the changes evident in the manifestation itself are small; when the number of causal changes increases, the changes can be world-changing in scope.

Everything is the result of the harmony between causes and conditions, from which all phenomena derive their mutable, impermanent, illusory and transient nature. The partial, relative perspective on this relationship considers that phenomena cease to be when the casual conditions producing them disperse. The holistic, absolute perspective, on the other hand, holds that phenomena do not vanish or disappear, they simply come apart, de-structure or dis-integrate and their constituent parts enter another material state. In fact, every phenomenon we perceive around us has evolved through composition after composition, beginning with the various fundamental elements that existed at the beginning of the universe, which themselves evolved from even earlier materials, to take the form we currently associate with it. This is a continuous, never-ending process. Every phenomenon is, therefore, at the moment of our perceiving it, simply manifesting one possible arrangement of the materials and causal conditions involved in its origination, at a single point in the timeline of the universe's development. It is limited to that point; it is an ephemeral manifestation. Essentially then, no phenomenon has a beginning or end.

The internal essence of phenomena determines they cannot exist in perpetuity. However, phenomena are not essentially void. They are not empty vessels. They do not blow in on the wind or appear out of thin air. They have an origin. They derive from the harmony of causes and conditions and manifest certain external forms, so they cannot be void or entirely non-existent.

Our self-nature of mind, too, is constantly changing and readily mutable. Its changeable nature provides a useful analogy for explaining 'existence' and 'non-existence' in a way that is easy to understand. Think of someone who is often warm toward you, but sometimes becomes mean. In their meanest moments, do you ever wonder if the warmth and gentleness you associate with them still exists? Of course you don't. Inevitably, when they return to being their lovely selves, you quickly embrace that version of them as their true self. We are talking about one person, who at different times and in different contexts acts either kind or mean. Which is their true self, and which the fake? We don't need to think hard to know these two kinds of behaviour or modes are simply distinct appearances or manifestations of the person, brought about by causal changes. Gentleness and meanness do not come out of nothing; and they do not last forever. This is Buddhist Dharma's insight into Emptiness.

In mundane society, it is our mind's habit to categorise anything 'present', substantial and therefore perceived, as 'existent'. We stand firm and clear when it comes to the existence or non-existence of phenomena. There is rarely any ambiguity around this question. A horse is a horse, a donkey a donkey; this is this and that is that. From our first days, we are always establishing our cognition of things – whether we think of this as real or fake, that as good or bad. Buddhist Dharma prescribes an entirely different approach to looking at the world: one of non-duality, according to which this contains that, and that contains this; one based on a fundamental knowledge about mutual interdependence. Dharma teaches us that phenomena are neither real nor unreal. They are the unreal within the real; the real within the unreal. There are no good or bad phenomena. There are only the bad within the good; the good within the bad. They do not truly 'exist', and they do not 'not-exist'. They lie in a state between 'existence' and 'non-existence'. The Buddha taught that any attachment to either 'existence' or 'non-existence' derives from a deluded view.

Notions of 'existence' or 'non-existence' easily lead to false understanding. The former engenders a view of the myriad things as having essentially permanent and independent existences; the latter, a view of everything as nothing, arisen out of thin air. Belief in either view only draws us further from realising the true nature of things. In order to dispel erroneous and deluded perspectives, we must establish a belief in essential 'impermanence' and 'non-self' – this is the correct view. Buddhist practitioners who have cultivated this perspective do not easily fall into the trap of deluded thinking and refuse to be led astray by facades of 'existence' and 'non-existence'. This is one of the most powerful teachings of the Dharma, that of the Middle Way and Middle View. The Buddha even advised that practitioners do not waste their time and energies debating these concepts of 'existence' and 'non-existence'. They are mere distractions from more pressing areas of study.

The priority is grasping the concept, 'everything is the result of the harmony of causes and conditions.' We, like the rest of the myriad things, both material and phenomenal, are the product of an ever-changing combination of causal factors, hence our own ever-changing manifestations and states. The various stages throughout that process of flux are what make up the stages of our life. Cause and effect determine how exactly those stages unfold. When we act correctly, we sow the causal seeds for good results, so when the time comes to reap the fruits of our actions, what we receive are what Dharma calls karmic rewards. Were our actions to run counter to the proper course of things, on the other hand, we would accumulate bad causal seeds, which only result in suffering – the retribution, as Buddhism calls it, that we deserve. Remember this: everything we have was received from causes and conditions. Nothing arises out of thin air, and nothing happens without a reason. Every phenomenon and manifestation can be traced back to its origins, to the causes and conditions that laid the grounds for its arising.

We laypeople are accustomed to looking first at the manifestations of things. It is not our habit to look to their essence. For this reason, we readily fall under the spell of their appearance. The wisdom of Dharma lies in how it guides us to maintain proper mindfulness and a right view, a right understanding, the right ideas and behaviours. Buddhist Dharma reminds us everything is the result of the harmony of causes and conditions and therefore lacks any eternal nature. It also reminds us that the manifestations of things are not non-existent or nothing. Based on the universal principle, the wisdom of Dharma can help free us from ignorance, confusion and attachment and liberate us from afflictions and suffering.

This year, I paid a visit to Weiming School in Guangzhou. There was a sign over the school sports track that caught my attention. It read, 'Weiming, where we seek out the fundamental laws of our world.' 'Ming', it occurred to me then, is the same 'ming' as is emphasised by the Dharma – knowing, understanding or clarity; for a school to base its teaching in the same quest 'for understanding' as Buddhism is impressive. If our children are already looking for the fundamental laws of our world in school, they have a strong chance of living free of ignorance and suffering later in life. Ignorance and suffering result from a lack of understanding of the essential principles of our world, whereas understanding puts us among the ranks of the Buddha, possessing the right view of 'impermanence' and 'non-self'. This view of things opens the window to seeing the true form of this worldly realm and to breaking free from our ignorance and suffering and to developing true wisdom.

CHAPTER THREE

The Essential Nature of the Myriad Things and Emptiness According to the Dharma

Form is emptiness'. Emptiness is the Buddha. Buddhist Dharma teaches that everything is empty. Specifically, that the true essence of all phenomena is emptiness.

The universe is in a constant state of change. It has never stopped expanding since its birth. Distant stars and planets continue to move away from us at high speed, some even faster than the speed of light. It is the law of the universe that everything within it, humans included, is bound to causal conditions, and we change as they do. In fact, the only constant is 'change' itself. We like change, because it means there is a chance for something better to come. We also fear change, because what follows might end up being worse than before. Our state of mind fluctuates in response to the inconsistent, often unpredictable, changes that unfold around us, unless, that is, we can settle our minds. But how do we do that? How do we reel in our thoughts? How do we resist the influence of external change in order to abide in a state of quiet and tranquillity? Buddhist Dharma holds the answers. Its wisdom is like a bamboo raft we can ride on to reach the other shore. It's like a compass pointing us in the right direction.

The prevalent view in society is that every person is an individual with a self-interested nature. What this view does not always acknowledge, however, is that that side of ourselves, the ego, is smart and cunning, driven by greed and wild desire. How we control, subdue and even cleanse ourselves of its influence is one of the most precious lessons Dharmic wisdom can teach us. Emptiness, it tells us, makes up the essential nature of the myriad things. So if we can understand our essential nature, we can understand Emptiness.

There are two sides to everything: its internal, essential nature and its external manifestation. Together, these two sides make a whole. Since everything is the result of the harmony of causes and conditions, and has no intrinsic essential substance, we can safely say that the essence of the myriad things is Emptiness. This is what Buddhist Dharma teaches us.

All phenomena lack inherent essential substance and self-existence. There are no independently existing phenomena in the world, and there never have been. Everything is formed of two or more elements and depends on the harmony and rearrangement of certain causes and conditions to manifest and change. This idea is the basis for the core teachings of the Dharma, which include the principle of cause and effect, Emptiness and nirvanic transcendence.

Phenomena are mutually interdependent for their existence and characteristics. One phenomenon is one of many causal conditions for another phenomenon's manifestation. How it combines with the other causal conditions and the results this alignment produces are indefinite and uncontrollable. They also shift constantly, causing the phenomenon to shift constantly as well. It is an unpredictable process, which Buddhist Dharma summarises as the impermanence of things – a lack of any fixed, unchanging state.

The Dharma identifies the cause of this mutability and reliance on external causes and conditions as the essential lack of any intrinsic, independent substance that can be associated with any individual phenomenon. In relative terms, phenomena only manifest an appearance for a short time, until shifts in their originary causal conditions make them take on new appearances. In absolute terms, phenomena exist in constant flux and can never manifest the whole range of their possible appearances at any one time. The names we use to distinguish them are nothing more than labels. Phenomena cannot exist forever and will sooner or later disintegrate, for their composite parts to form something new. So, although they are essentially emptiness, phenomena do not derive from nothingness; they have an origin.

While manifestations of things have characteristics that our eyes, ears, tongue, nose, skin and mind can perceive, the Dharma teaches us that their essential nature is Emptiness. They possess no intrinsic self. This is why the myriad things do not experience suffering. Their resulting impermanence allows phenomena infinite possibilities for how they manifest.

We know now the truth of the origin and essence of the cosmos and its contents. It is a truth the Buddha discovered 2600 years and which remains true even today. So, you're probably wondering how the Buddha uncovered it and why he renounced his princely status to become a monk and dedicate himself to pursuing the path to liberation – the Way. And how that led to him becoming the Buddha. His story is one Buddhist practitioners of every level should know.

The Buddha, named Siddhārtha Gautama and also Shakyamuni, was born a prince around 2600 years ago in Kapilavastu, ancient India. Early on, Siddhārtha displayed a preternatural intelligence and diverse abilities far beyond what is ordinary. At fifteen, he started to read religious and philosophical texts and to pay regular visits to the city's priests and brahmans with his fellow students. Monks had by then begun to advocate leaving home, relinquishing all worldly affairs and going in search of the Way to liberation from suffering, a way of life and a quest Siddhārtha eventually took on. He was influenced to do so by the experiences he had on the three occasions that he snuck out of the palace. The first time he time he slipped out of the palace, he met a person struggling with sickness; the second time he saw a doddering old woman, stooped over and shuffling along and the third time he saw people carrying a dead body. Each of the visits rocked Siddhārtha even more than the last, as he tried to come to terms with the inevitable suffering humans faced in their lives – sickness, ageing and death. He also witnessed other unspeakably tragic scenes: malnourished children as thin as matchsticks, beggars limping through crowds, workers ground down by poverty and labour. Siddhārtha knew that even though he was set to inherit the throne, it would be difficult for him to make any real change from there. He would also have no freedom as a ruler, so he decided to leave the palace to search of the path to liberation from suffering – the Way. He had realised the luxurious palace life could only ever provide a temporary kind of happiness and suffering would sooner or later find him as well. So, in an act of great compassion, he dedicated himself to discovering how to release all sentient beings from their terrible fate.

Siddhārtha spent years cultivating the Way, discovering the greatest truths in the smallest details and the subtlest lessons in the largest things. He observed the whole of the universe in every cell of his body; that a speck of dust was the cosmos itself and held the truth to everything. He experienced a great awakening. He sat to meditate beneath the Bodhi tree and he realised 'everything is the result of the combination of two or more elements' and the myriad things, void of any intrinsic self-existence, are mutually interdependent for their manifestation. He found that everything is, at its core, Emptiness and any belief to the contrary, in the existence of 'eternal and constant' manifestations 'possessed of a self', is the source of all humanity's suffering. He knew, then, what the key to liberation is: alignment with the essential 'impermanence' and 'non-self' of things. He achieved enlightenment. After many years of cultivation, Siddhārtha, now the Buddha, finally realised the fundamental principle of how to attain freedom from suffering, which he designed the Dharma around.

Just to note, when in this book it says everything is dependent on the harmony of causes and conditions to manifest, the 'everything' in question refers to all phenomena – events, things, people – in the universe, but does not include the essential nature of those phenomena, because that is absolute, unconditional, immutable. For humans, this essential absence of intrinsic self-existence, this non-self, is our Buddha nature. This is the universal principle.

The essential nature of the myriad things is consistent across all time and space. If you know what lies at the core of the universe, you also know what is immanent within everything it contains – the true and substantial form of things. This core aspect never increases or decreases. It never starts or ceases. It is neither pure nor impure. It simply is. This truth serves as the basis for all of the teachings of the Dharma. It is the truth of Emptiness

Buddhist scriptures relate the story of when the bodhisattva Manjushri asked the Buddha, 'What is the true form of phenomena?' In response to the question, rather than give a direct answer, the Buddha slipped into meditation, leaving the crowd looking around at each other wondering what was happening. What was the Buddha trying to tell them? Right then, Manjushri had an epiphany. The Buddha is Emptiness, and Emptiness is the Buddha. The true form of phenomena is Emptiness – an intrinsic lack of self-existence.

Absolute Emptiness defies easy description and is a challenge for us to consider in either emotional or theoretical terms. If it wasn't, surely the Buddha's reply to Manjushri would have been simply to show him, 'This is their true form.' But had he done that it would not have been pure Emptiness he was describing. The kind of Emptiness we can describe with language is simply conceptual, it is not Emptiness itself. So instead of answering Majushri's question with words, the Buddha entered into a meditative state, to show his disciple that this is the absolute true form of things, this is Emptiness.

Indeed, Emptiness can only be sensed or felt. It is something we must grasp intuitively. If someone asks you to describe a flower, I imagine you would be able to do so quite well, especially if you are allowed to us modern technology, to take and show a photograph, for example. But were someone to ask you to describe the essential nature of that flower, I suspect you couldn't. The essential nature of a thing sits within it. If we can perceive this nature, then what we see might well differ from what someone else sees or senses, perhaps by quite a lot, for that matter. But if we can't, then we can't. But either way, language cannot capture the essential nature of a flower; it is insufficient, incomprehensible, limited in its scope. Both the essential nature of things and Emptiness must therefore be intuited.

However, we have to start somewhere, so here I will give a short explanation of the concept of Emptiness. What is Emptiness? And why the name, Emptiness? 'Emptiness' – or 'a nature of Emptiness' as is the more literal translation of the equivalent Chinese word *kongxing* 空性 – derives from the Sanskrit *Śūnyatā* (or 'shunyata'). *'Kong'* 空 can mean a multitude of things in Chinese, depending on the context, though it consistently has spatial connotations. As I understand it, Buddhist Dharma regards Emptiness as the nature of all things; it is a quiddity of constant value; it never increases or decreases, never arises or ceases, it is neither pure nor impure – it is eternal. The choice of label for this quality, Emptiness, derives from the intrinsic absence of any self-nature within the myriad things. They are empty of an independent self-existence. At their core, they are non-self.

Emptiness indicates causality and conditionality – a fate of endless and unavoidable transformation. The secular view of things is that everything only exists for a short time. The Dharmic perspective is that nothing really exists; everything only manifests for a time. Ultimately and fundamentally, nothing can exist forever, since nothing meets the Dharma's standard for 'existence'. All conditioned phenomena are like dreams or illusions. At their core, they are empty.

What is existence? For the Dharma, it is anything that is independent in its being and evolution, anything that is eternal. So, the only thing that exists is the essential nature of phenomena – in our case that is our intrinsic nature of non-self, also known as Buddha nature. The world, the cosmos – as big as they are and with all they contain, there is nothing else with eternal existence.

Everything is the result of the harmony of causes and conditions; such is the universal principle around which Buddhist Dharma centres and upon which the right view of 'impermanence' and 'non-self' is based. Intuitive experience of this perspective of things reveals that neither the controversial concept of 'existence' or 'non-existence' aligns with the universal principle. They both derive from extreme standpoints. Buddhist Dharma takes the Middle Way between these two extremes and teaches that the myriad things neither exist in perpetuity nor arise out of nothingness. They sit somewhere between existence and non-existence.

This state is determined by the myriad things' reliance on causes and conditions to manifest. Since the possible combinations of causes and conditions are infinite, there are infinite possibilities for how phenomena might manifest. Often, they do so in ways that defy our expectations. What's more, how we perceive their manifestation tends to differ between different people, since we each have our own perspectives, life experiences and self-conceit to base our interpretations on.

It is a well-known saying from Buddhism that everything is a manifestation of the mind. Since everyone's mind is in a state of its own at any one time, what we perceive and how we perceive it differs from person to person. Buddhist Dharma reminds us that in different contexts, at different times, things take on different appearances. We have no way of seeing the whole range of a phenomenon's potential manifestations all at once; we can only ever see the part that is manifest when we are paying attention. Therefore, we must not become attached to our perceptions. Perception is conditional, and what we see under specific causal conditions is not the true form of a thing. As the Diamond Sutra says, 'All phenomena that have characteristics are illusory and ephemeral. When one realizes that perceived ideas are not concretely real, then one sees Tathâgata [the true suchness of things].' We must remember we can only see one side or one aspect of things.

There is one more important property of phenomena we need to examine, and that is 'non-duality' – equality both across states and between distinct phenomena. Like non-self, it is a very challenging Dharmic concept to grasp.

In the world view of Dharma, 'singularity' indicates a lack of differentiation between things, while 'duality' implies differentiation. So, viewing the myriad things with a non-differentiating perspective or intent, and treating them equally, means we are operating, conceptually speaking, in a 'singular', or 'non-dualistic', cognitive mode. Otherwise, we are prone to differentiation and 'dualistic' thinking. We should not underestimate 'non-dualistic' thinking, even if it is difficult to understand based on our ordinary experiences and ego-driven state of mind.

To assist us, let's consider it from a more suitable perspective – one centred around the idea of collective existence and derived from non-self. As far as the universe is concerned, every manifestation of every phenomenon is equally important. Had an asteroid not crashed into Earth 6500 years ago, causing volcanoes to erupt and bringing out a catastrophic shift in the climate, wiping out the dinosaurs which had ruled the planet for a hundred million years, then just maybe those dinosaurs would still be at the top of the food chain, and humans might never have evolved. It makes no difference to the universe whether it is us or the dinosaurs who live today. There is no differentiating between which is good and which is bad. Both situations are simply the result of the harmony of causes and conditions.

Buddhist Dharma reminds us that things take on different appearances in different contexts and at different times. We have no way of seeing the whole range of a phenomenon's potential manifestations all at once; we can only ever see the part that is manifest when we are paying attention. Therefore, we must not become attached to our perceptions. ▶▶

So, non-dualistic thinking means an absence of differentiation: no discrimination between large and small, good and bad, benevolent and evil, clean and dirty, gains and losses, success and failure, richness and poverty. If we pay attention, it quickly becomes obvious how attached we are to the values we have been forming since our childhoods; when they are rocked or receive a blow, our ego's reflex is to jump to the defence of our interests. As a result, the majority of us laypeople struggle not to weigh up our successes and failures, to compare the haves and have-nots. We might manage to avoid making these kinds of calculations for a very limited selection of things, but if we want to avoid them outright, we must foster non-dualistic thinking. We have to go with the flow, in a sense; embrace the essential nature of the myriad things. We must align ourselves with non-self.

At the moment, dualistic thinking is second nature to most of us. It is deeply ingrained within our psyche; it is our default mode. Not long after we were born, we started to form our model of subjective thinking. We quickly became the sole agent in our lives, and from then on the world and its contents seemed centred around us. Everything exterior to us became an object in our eyes. That is dualistic thinking, a product of the human mind if there ever was one. But it is only natural that dualistic thinking follows the conception of the self. Alignment with non-self means non-dualistic thought can occur. As has been mentioned above, every phenomenon is dependent on an immeasurable number of causes and conditions for its manifestation and is, at the same time, itself a causal condition for the manifestation of other phenomena. Soil, moisture, heat, a seed, a tree, the sun, rain, time, space – these are all necessary elements for a leaf to grow. Were one of them removed, the leaf could not grow. In this sense, soil, moisture and sunlight are all of equal importance to the leaf, such is the integrated nature of the universe and the myriad things; seeing things as such is one example of non-dualistic thinking or thinking about Emptiness. Non-dualistic thought recognises every individual phenomenon within the universe as part of the collective whole, with each part equal to every other part. Any comparison between any two elements is invalid.

No differentiation can be made and there are no antithetical relationships between the composite parts. Everything is as it should be according to the natural course of its causal conditions.

There is no subject-object relationship, no big and small, no good and bad, no pure and impure. These are all human concepts, the products of a differentiating mind. Dualistic thought divides the whole into parts, and in doing so, permits us to see only one side of things, which we very quickly become used to seeing exclusively. We have a knack for it, for associating with the aspect we are most familiar with or the one we most want to see, while the rest become unclear, or even invisible, to us, and we are hindered from seeing the true form or nature of that thing.

Rather than settling with the dualistic way of thinking which our self-centred nature habituates us to, we should aim to foster non-dualistic thinking, as prescribed by the Dharma. All phenomena are interdependent and interconnected. There is no such thing as absolute good or absolute bad. Good and bad simply exist as constituents of a thing, as two sides of the same coin, so to speak. Non-dualistic thinking lies at the heart of Buddhism's wisdom about Emptiness. It reveals the extent of the power of non-self, since removing subjectivity from our cognition is the key to no longer differentiating between things − between good and bad; between degrees of importance; between you and me. Accepting our causes and conditions, or rather, accepting origination, then becomes easy, because without differentiation, we do not develop attachments. Without attachments, we do not fall into affliction or suffering.

The phenomena we become attached to are only ephemeral manifestations in the first place. Specifically, they are manifestations of our disposition toward the things, events or ideas we associate with the phenomenon in question. What we perceive is not the true phenomenon, it is not even the true, unadulterated manifestation of that phenomenon. We each have our unique dispositions, so our perceptions are unique as well. The Buddha once taught his followers that we must maintain a modest and open mind, and strive at all times to get to the bottom of our experiences and perceptions. This is the only way we can ever gain a comprehensive cognition and understanding of things and a closer view of their true form.

For our purposes, we should think of phrases like 'essential nature', 'true form' and Emptiness as synonymous. Perceiving the essential nature of a thing is equivalent to perceiving its true form, which in line with the universal is Emptiness. If we are blind to one of them, we are blind to all of them. I remember a scene in a film in which a young person asks a monk, 'What is ignorance?' The monk replies, 'Seeing the world around you but failing to see its true form.' The youth says, 'I have eyes and ears, how can I not see?' The monk answers, 'You have been blinded by your attachments, so you cannot see the true form of the world.'

The world is layered. There is the material, phenomenal layer, which most of us focus on day to day. It is what we perceive with our eyes, the superficial level of things. Dharma points us to the abstract layer, which is the intrinsic, essential nature of all phenomena – the truth beneath the illusion. Ignorance is when we are convinced the superficial layer is the real thing, to the extent we cannot perceive the essential nature of the universe – impermanence and non-self. This is how Buddhism sees it. For Buddhism, the essential nature of things is most important.

Setbacks can drop the unprepared into a labyrinth of fear; but those of us who study and practice the Dharma know everything is the product of the harmony of causes and conditions and when a thing's origination changes, so does the thing. We are prepared in this knowledge. ▶▶

What good does it us, though, to acknowledge the intrinsic nature of things? What is so important about recognising impermanence and non-self? Why must we start from these qualities when we move about in this world? For those of us wanting to foster a deeper understanding of Buddhist Dharma and even cultivate a Dharmic practice, these are questions that require constant reflection and probing. Insight into the myriad things' impermanence and non-self is the confidence boost we need in order to feel certain we can rid ourselves of afflictions and suffering. But the question is: are we ready to accept the universal principle? Are we willing to embrace the true form of things?

We seldom acknowledge the impermanence of things in our daily lives, if we believe in it at all. In particular, we fail to remember our own impermanence. This essential characteristic is intrinsic to us as well as to the external world; we exist in perpetual change. We must bear this in mind. Even those of us who have accepted impermanence, both our own and that of things other than ourselves, only do so to a certain degree. We have our own standards for what we believe a demonstration of impermanence to be. We tend only to accept it when it falls within what we consider to be a rational scope. Whenever that is the case, we feel at ease. But when impermanence defies our expectations, when our predefined standard is violated, we take it as a significant blow and lose our presence of mind, so we feel at a loss or even hopeless. We have experienced a display of impermanence in action we cannot accept, and unless we change our attitude, the result can be unspeakable suffering.

Aligning ourselves with the non-self nature of the myriad things also presents problems. In fact, processing the concept of non-self alone is difficult, especially when we have to try and come to terms with our own non-self. Living in harmony with the non-self of the world around us while simultaneously and consistently embodying it ourselves presents an intimidating challenge. This is one of the most difficult parts of Buddhist practice. It cannot be hurried. There are steps we must take to gradually sharpen our awareness before we can create the circumstances necessary for us to embody our nature of non-self, at first partially, then wholly.

None of us is resistant to sudden changes occurring in our origination and bringing about a seismic shift in our circumstances, whether that be for better or worse. So it is imperative that we remain aware at all times, like a gazelle, of the possibility of change and make the necessary psychological preparations to face such impermanence. That way we can avoid or resolve any crises. Without that kind of awareness and vigilance, there is a chance we will become passive in our lives as well, pulled in the direction change dictates rather than the one we decide. We must learn from the life experiences of countless other people before us, who have, after accumulating years of bad karma or being struck by tragedy, been gripped by debilitating fear or panic and been left unsure how to go on; or who have, in an instant, been dropped into a labyrinth of terror, one which takes a very long time to escape from. Lots of people scramble about for a way to alleviate their fear, but they rarely succeed in any significant way. The repercussions of living in fear for a prolonged time are hard to imagine.

Thankfully, we all find the Dharma sooner or later. If we have the great fortune for that to come in this life so we can start our practice now, then it will not be long before the truth of dependent origination will become clear – an early wake up call to snap us out of our slumberous lives. Either way, in studying the Dharma, we learn to recognise the source of our pain and not to let it return, to start afresh and plan for a new future, to rid ourselves of our afflictions, once and for all, and develop bodhi wisdom. Then there will be nothing to be afraid of. Each of the myriad things has its rightful place and path. Faced with great setbacks, it is best to turn to reflection and change; not fear.

If we want guidance on how to embody non-self and embrace impermanence, we should follow the example of the Buddha. He dedicated most of his life to helping others find liberation from suffering and attain Buddhahood. The Buddhist doctrine of Emptiness was the Buddha's core tool for guiding them down this

this path. At the heart of that teaching is the idea of non-self. The best method for embodying non-self is by helping others. The more that we help others, the easier it is to realise our nature of non-self.

A disciple once asked the Buddha, 'Liberation is achieved by seeing the true form of things. Does it not matter how we manage that? Whether by performing our duties, worship or chanting scripture?' The Buddha explained, 'Imagine a person who wants to cross a river. If the water is shallow, they can wade across. If the water is deep, they might need to swim or take a boat. But if that person never steps into the water or onto a boat, choosing instead to stand on the bank and pray they might one day reach the other bank, do you think that will get them very far? If you do not remove the barrier of ignorance from your path, even if you spend your whole life in prayer, then all your efforts will be in vain. Only by seeing to the core of phenomena, to the universal nature within them, can we escape the grip of ignorance. Ignorance is the source of all suffering.'

It is ignorance of our non-self we most need to leave behind. It is thanks to their essential nature of non-self that the myriad things of the universe display no trace of suffering, whereas we humans, with our ego-driven minds and eagerness to differentiate, suffers through much of our lives. This is despite the countless experiences we have that point us to one key truth: as long as there is a 'self', there will be suffering. And the stronger our attachment to that notion of 'self', the more intense the suffering.

Here, it is important to remind you that there is a difference between discerning the true nature of things – non-self, impermanence, Emptiness – and the actual essential qualities themselves. The first is changeable and dependent on origination, while the latter are eternal and immutable. For example, we might have insight into non-self but still not be able to embody non-self in our actions; we might possess insight into impermanence but still fcling to expectations and attachments. Thinking about an ideal and embodying it are two matters entirely. To convert insight into realisation, well, that is the greatest challenge there is.

The *Diamond Sutra* contains the Buddha's explanation about the external appearance of things not being their natural state. 'All phenomena that have characteristics are illusory and ephemeral. When one realizes that perceived ideas are not concretely real, then one sees Tathâgata [the true suchness of things].'

After the Buddha realised the universal principle and how to achieve liberation from suffering, as he sat beneath the Bodhi tree, he decided to design a set of teachings to guide others to that same realisation. These teachings are what make up Buddhist Dharma. He also created the Sangha, a community of students and followers dedicated to the path he laid out for them with the Dharma. The Buddha said that monks must take refuge in the Three Jewels: the Buddha, the Dharma, and the Sangha. A monk's first duty is to invest their whole self, body and mind, into realising liberation. Then they should aid others in doing the same. Liberation refers specifically to liberation from suffering, which requires seeing to the intrinsic essence of things, beneath their superficial appearances, as the Buddha did. We must realise the non-self within us and all other phenomena, the essence of our mind, our Buddha nature and Emptiness. These insights will allow us to abide in our natural state of mind, which is the armour we need to become resistant to the influence of the external world. By transcending the self, we embody non-self and realise the Buddha nature within our mind. As the Buddha said, a mind possessed of Buddha nature is a liberated mind.

CHAPTER FOUR

The Self- and Non-Self Nature of Mind

In relative terms, the human mind has two modes: the non-self nature of mind, which is centred around collective existence, and the self-nature of mind, which assumes the individual to be the at the centre of all things. In absolute terms, the notion of a mind in the first place is man-made, invented for the sake of convenience. Really the myriad things possess a single, intrinsic, essential nature. For humans, that essential nature is the non-self nature of mind – Buddha nature.

As far as we know, the universe and its contents contain the whole of existence. All of space and time, material and energy are contained within the universe. Without the universe, there would be no Earth; without Earth, there would be no humankind; without humans, we would not believe in the existence of any individual self. The universe represents collective existence.

The origination of the universe and its contents occurs in accordance with the continuous and ever-shifting alignment of causal and conditional elements. Primary among them are the causes that lead to origination; secondary are the conditions. Their particular combination at any given moment engenders the form or changes we perceive – or don't – in that moment. These three elements form the working heart of the law of cause and effect – causes, conditions and harmony.

After the Big Bang but before galaxies took shape, before the sun had formed and before the planet we rely on for life existed, origination was still unfolding. Diverse and constant shifts and alignments in causes and conditions were occurring, which eventually led to the formation of our galaxy, the sun and the planets including the Earth. From nothing but a desolate rock, the Earth gained splendid mountains and rivers, lush, green grass and life burgeoning in countless forms. Everything we know resulted from transformations prompted by the innumerable instances of origination all that time ago. In the early millennia of Earth, there was magma, stone and soil. Later, water and seas appeared. Then organisms, like plants and animals, and eventually humans. If the stone, soil, flora and fauna preceded humans, does that mean we too evolved from them? In *Old Path White Clouds*, the Buddha tells some children, "We have all existed in times before there were humans, or even birds and mammals on Earth. There were only plants beneath the seas, trees and other plants on the Earth's surface. In those times we may have been stones, dew, or plants. Afterwards we experienced lives as birds, as all kinds of animals, and finally as human beings." The earth resembles a speck of dust in the grand scope of the universe, and human beings represent much the same on the surface of Earth. Seen from an absolutist point of view, humans are nothing but one kind of material form among many; we are just another composite part of Earth, alongside sand and stones. There is no difference between us and them. It is important we acknowledge this relationship to the universe and to the myriad things. It is also important we realise the only thing that differentiates us from the rest of the myriad things is our mind-nature.

Humankind as a whole has a reasonable understading of Earth and the Solar System. But our understanding of the galaxies beyond ours is limited, to say the least. There is much we know of recent history, but much we do not know of the origins of humankind and the times before that. Research into the structure of the human body is comprehensive, but there is a lot we still need to learn about the immaterial aspect of the brain and the mind. These are gaping holes in our knowledge which we would benefit from filling in, but in the meantime it is fortunate we can feel certain about one important aspect of the mind and our origins: there is a special connection between the human mind and the collective existence of the universe. From my own experience I can say with some confidence that within the human mind there are two sides working against one another: that of "non-self", which views the world through the lens of collective existence, and that of "self", which manifests as conviction in individual, independent existence. However, it bears repeating that this is a relative perspective of the mind. Conversely, Buddhism sees the universe in absolutes and recognises the human mind is an artificial concept, a convenient label. The truth is that all things possess a single, intrinsic, essential nature, which for humans is our nature of non-self, our Buddha nature.

Why do human beings innately possess a nature of non-self? The answer can be found in the universal principle. Everything originates from the material that existed at the beginning of the universe, which was itself formed of causes and conditions. Humans are no different.

We are the result of the origination that has driven all change since then. Our "existence" is dependent. Therefore, we, like the myriad things, lack any independent, intrinsic nature of self. Rather, we are imbued with non-self, always have been and always will be.

This immanent non-self derives a sense of identity from where it fits within collective existence and centres on the present moment. It is imbued with reverence for the myriad things and aims to serve the universe as a whole. It is the source of our kind-heartedness. It is what guides us to compassion and love in how we treat and view others. It is their essential non-self that keeps the myriad things free from attachments and, in turn, free from suffering. It is our Buddha nature that is awake to these aspects of our being. To tap into our Buddha nature is to transcend ignorance, to live free from attachments and suffering, to be able to abide in a state of tranquillity and calm.

Non-self is immanent within all of us. It is our intrinsic Buddha Nature, our essential harmony with collective existence, our source of reverence for the myriad things and a wellspring of compassion and love. ▶▶

Of course, these terms, as with every term, are inventions by humans. They only serve as tools for us to identify and distinguish the world around us. They are insufficient to capture the full essence of a thing, but they allow us at least to begin to make out its shape. Another term we must grasp is "collective existence". The universe is a kind of collective existence. There may be universes outside of this universe, and all these universes, when seen together, may be said to represent collective existence. Or we can choose to treat Earth and everything on it as a form of collective. Or a certain area of Earth and its contents; or everything within the scope of our perception and cognition. Really, anything larger than an individual unit can be considered for a particular purpose a collective whole. It is a relative term. It is even our habit to view ourselves as the centre of all things, a habit we foster from our first moments alive onward. But we must strive to establish an intimate understanding of our place within collective existence if we hope to weaken our self-centredness and embody our nature of non-self.

Collective existence refers to all of natural existence combined. Space, the sky, the ground, mountains and rivers, trees and other plants, animals, whether landbound or winged – they, along with everything else, make up collective existence. So, in a sense, anything greater than the individual is a manifestation of collective existence and requires our respect. We should try to co-exist in harmony with the collective around us in the present moment. It is our nature to do so. When we manifest our nature of non-self, we become consciously connected to and resonate with the present moment and collective existence.

When our self-centred, individualist aspect is in control, our lives become dominated by ego. We spend our days in a world of our own imagining, in our own thoughts, oblivious of all other concerns but our own. We sever our connection with collective existence. We abandon the present moment. Our ego suppresses our nature of non-self and casts us in the leading role of the universe and everything else as subject to us. Our ego dictates our temperament and our reactions to any change and orgination, breeding antagonism and resistance. Everything causes us suffering. Just as Bodhidharma says in the Treatise on Contemplating Mind, "All others, trapped by the impure mind and entangled by their own karma, are mortals. They drift through the three realms and suffer countless afflictions and all because their impure mind obscures their real self."

Most of us would be lucky if we lived for a hundred years, a period which Buddhism regards as a single cycle of life and death. It is natural for us to have a self-nature of mind; it is something humans always have through every cycle of life and death. Every being has its unique qualities and individual characteristics, and an individual self-nature of mind is innate to humans. This is the relative view of things.

Indeed, Buddhism disregards the self-nature of sentient beings as innate. It is acquired, the Dharma tells us, as the result of causes and conditions after birth. So, if we nurture our ego and consolidate our sense of being an individual self, our ego will only become more extreme. But this of course means that the reverse is also true: we can weaken our ego, even to the point of powerlessness, when we will resemble the bodhisattvas of legend who were awake to Emptiness. Other names for the self or ego include the empirical self, the conditioned self and the unreal self. Buddhist Dharma teaches us the self is nothing more than a surface phenomenon we conceive of ourselves. We must see through such illusions to the intrinsic quality of people and things.

Our relationship with surface phenomena can be summarised as a constant search, shared by all individuals, for how best to maximise our personal interests, trying to satisfy our needs and increase our enjoyment. We amass knowledge, qualifications, skills and networks by every means possible in order to increase our own personal resources and we compete with others to ensure we have the advantage. This kind of competition is fertile ground for growing our conception of our self and, in doing so, blocking out our nature of non-self nature. Frequently ignored, frequently dismissed, our immanent non-self is the side of our psyche we readily neglect and even bury deep down. Like tarnished gold, its value becomes unclear. The *Three Character Classic* reads, "Humans are born benevolent and alike in nature; it is through habit that their natures start to diverge." This explains how it is our nature to be kind-hearted in our early years, yet later on in life we lose some, or even all of, that goodness.

Earth follows an orbit which obeys the celestial movements of the rest of the universe. This is harmony within a collective existence; with one's origination. Collective existence is at every moment changing in accordance with its shifting causes and conditions, this is how it evolved from its past iteration to its current one, and how it will become the collective existence of the future. We are forever bound to change as it unfolds over time and are an inextricable part of the present collective existence. Earth is bound to the universe as the individual is to the collective, just as we too are bound to the Earth and to the universe as a whole, except we are an even smaller part of that whole. If we wish to align ourselves with collective existence, embodying our non-self is a vital first step. We individual entities should serve the collective, respect the collective and be grateful to the collective for our part in it.

We individuals need to remind ourselves that everything we have comes from collective existence. Everything we possess or know is a gift from collective existence. None of it is really ours, it is only temporarily in our possession, and we should share it, rather than hog it greedily. Before perceiving and realizing our nature of mind can happen for us, we must establish an awareness of the collective and our place within it. The core lesson of the Chan teachings is how to realise one's non-self. "This [Buddha-] nature is mind; the mind is Buddha" (Bodhidharma, Treatise on the Transmission). We need to turn our awareness inward, toward our inner mind and being, and shine its light on the depths of our nature of non-self. There we will find our true self, our true nature. Our natural being represents a perfect marriage of the self and the collective. Alignment with it brings us to a state charged with the lifeforce, energy, contentment and tranquillity of our inner being.

50

Collective existence includes everything and everything belongs to collective existence. So anything we believe we possess, in truth, we are only looking after for a time. The notion of everlasting ownership derives from selfish, egotistical thinking, which the Dharma dismisses as deluded. The Buddha said that attachment to "permanence" and the "self" is the fundamental cause of all suffering. We suffer because of our conviction in the existence of a "self", which leads to differentiating, dualistic thinking, to attachments and to expectations. Suffering is a warning sign we are in conflict with collective existence and the essential nature of the myriad things.

In *Old Path White Clouds* the Buddha is recorded to have once said: "…births and deaths [are] but outward appearances and not true reality, just as millions of waves rise and fall incessantly on the surface of the sea, while the sea itself is beyond birth and death. If the waves understood that they themselves were water, they would transcend birth and death and arrive at true inner peace, overcoming all fear." It is true that when a wave – an individual – rejects being led astray by surface appearances and discovers her true nature, she will be able to transcend fear and find peace.

This is also a helpful metaphor for reminding us that we individuals are waves, if not mere drops of water, in the ocean of collective existence. A single wave or drop of water follows the ocean's will and abides by the ocean's laws and rhythm. It goes with the flow of the ocean. In doing so, it is doing as nature intends it and is thus embodying "non-self".

By contrast, self-centredness, a refusal to follow and serve and respect collective existence, cleaving to one's own way of thinking, one of antagonism and contradiction – this way of being can only lead to suffering.

So, the individual and the collective share a relationship of reverence and service while individuals have more of a friendship, one of amity, acceptance, respect and love. Kind-heartedness, modesty, courtesy and compassionate love all count among the qualities immanent within non-self. They are the qualities of Buddha-nature, which every one of us is born with. We all possess them, our children more clearly than the rest of us. It is owing to our habits we have cultivated since birth that these qualities have become harder to tap into.

A manifest non-self is truly a powerful thing. Not only does it promise a peaceful, contended life, it also gives comfort to the people around you. Unsurprisingly, the inverse happens when it is our ego that stands at the fore of our mind. We scheme every day about how to satisfy our own desires. We focus only on ourselves. This world is everybody's to live in, so what makes us think we have the privilege to stand at the centre of it? Believing this inevitably results in an attitude of antagonism, which, in turn, brings about suffering for both ourselves and those around us. We reap what we sow. That is the simplest form of cause and effect. The Buddha said it best: if we show love and compassion to others, then they will reciprocate that love and compassion. If we are ruthless toward others, they will be ruthless in return. Mutual love and care are key ingredients for mutual harmony.

We should aim to treat others how we treat ourselves. Cultivating this approach to life and our environment is a key practice for Buddhists, which produces a state of being absent any notion of or distinction between subject and object, free of dualistic differentiation. All we have in life is our independence to make decisions ourselves, but that does not make us superior to other individuals. All people are equal. It is the equality of our natures that makes harmony between us possible.

Scientists have observed that the process of material phenomena moving from a state of "disorderliness" to one of "orderliness" requires the acquisition of energy. The reverse – entropy – is a process of energy expenditure. Our growth from birth onwards into adulthood follows a tendency toward "orderliness", as we gain energy from our environment. Maybe, the most efficient mode of being throughout this process is one of self-centredness. Of course, there are people who take that to a greater extreme than others. The degree to which we are selfish is determined by our origination.

We can trace our ego back to the moment of our birth, our mind begins to form and officially establishes our notion of our being or having a "self". I am me and you are you, and we are different – this is one of its first acts of differentiation. Then, I am more important than you, I am the centre of things, I am the world; the world is mine. At this point, our dualistic thinking is well on the way to solidifying. I am the subject, the actor, and everything external to me is an object. Then follow the evaluations of good and bad, the expectations and, ultimately, the attachments. The self, dualistic thinking, attachments, these concepts are all cut from the same cloth, they are links in a chain which locks us into certain behaviours. They are the root of afflictions and suffering.

Like any other animal, humans are subject to influence by their environment. So self-interest is in many ways a kind of defence mechanism. For the young, selfishness means a better chance of survival – it is instive. Some scientists say a child will get closest to whoever can provide them with milk, and there is data to prove it. Self-centredness, then, is one of the essential characteristics of the human mind. Although only young, children have a strong sense of self-preservation. If someone takes a child's toys, they will cry and have a tantrum. Such begins a lifetime habit of feeding our self-nature of mind until it is plump and fat, and shadows our non-self.

This is a process we should learn to control as soon as possible before we slip into extreme levels of selfishness. Extremely self-centred behaviour manifests differently in different people; it also manifests differently at different stages of our lives and in different contexts. As infants, if something goes against our wishes, we might hit our parents or grandparents or whoever is around us. Or if we see something we like we might try and hog that thing all for ourselves. If we don't get our way, we will whine and kick up a fuss and maybe roll around on the ground in protest. At school age, we might bully our weaker classmates, take advantage of others, fight or wrestle, and use aggressive means to take others' things. In the world of work, we could do whatever we can to get ahead, gamble, make money in illicit ways and bully our competitors. In old age, greed or miserliness are often how it manifests, whether that be with regard others or ourselves. We also fall into close-minded, stubborn, peremptory and intolerant ways of being. Extreme selfishness can manifest in countless different ways, and self-centredness of a lesser degree in even more diverse ways than that. A person at their most selfish will frequently wander into immoral territory with their actions and sometimes even break the law.

It only takes one or two people acting selfishly for a family, neighbourhood or work team to fall into disarray. Selfishness breeds trouble. It feeds on turning mountains into molehills and making problems out of nothing. Escalation is the aim of its game, and ruining happiness and dragging everyone else down its victory. At the other end of the spectrum, complete selflessness is based on giving: warmth, joy and a sense of belonging are among its best gifts.

The more self-centred an individual is, the further that individual will stray from alignment with the essential nature of the myriad things, and the more they will suffer. The more selfless an individual is, the more closely in line with the essential nature of the myriad things their life will be, and the lighter and freer they will feel. The earlier we realise this and begin our Buddhist practice, the sooner we can achieve liberation from suffering. The moment we realign ourselves with collective existence is the moment our path toward spiritual emancipation begins.

There are several billion people living on this planet, each one with a unique situation, which is the nature of being an individual. How we navigate that situation is guided by some manifestation of our self-nature. We each possess and foster in ourselves different qualities to other people. There are no two people on this planet who are exactly the same. For that reason, no one but ourselves can fully understand us inside and out.

It is important we practice awareness of our two natures. Slipping too far into individualism and forgetting about our non-self risks us becoming blind to that part of us, dooming us to selfishness and egotism. We have to nurture both sides so as to unlock our true selves and experience the true meaning of life.

The self and non-self can coexist within a person. In fact, harmony between them is what we consider the manifestation of our true selves. Whether or not we can tap into that state is determined by whether or not we are aware of our inner nature. Awareness is to the first step to having an awakening and attaining Buddhahood.

The idea of our true self being a balance between our two natures is popular in ordinary society, especially among young people, because it allows us to retain some degree of individuality. It is important, though, we understand the differences between the concepts of "true self" and "non-self". As far as I know, the true self is a manifestation of our being that remains tied to the mundane world. While an achievement in itself, it is only the first milestone in our cultivation. Completely embodying our nature of non-self brings about an absolute change. It is the ultimate goal of cultivation.

In perceiving and realising our mind-nature and in returning to our true self is contained the knowledge we need to embrace our origination, to live in the present and to know how to move through this world. A thoroughly selfless person is free. Their heart is full of peace and joy, love and compassion. There are countless practitioners who can tell us from experience that the more ego-driven we are, the more attachments we develop, while the more selfless we are, the fewer attachments we have. For a person who clings to their notion of selfhood, death is a terrifying prospect. And it remains so for anyone who has already embodied their true self. Only for the practitioner who has fully awoken to their nature of non-self is death not a fearsome prospect.

There is a lot about ourselves and our lives we know like the back of our hands. But when it comes to our inner selves, our knowledge barely scratches the surface. Our mission in life should be to excavate – to discover who we truly are. But for most of us that is a distant goal. We are lost in the sea of our own desires. Ego undeniably breeds desire. Its main aim is to maximise its own interests, which leads to constantly chasing new goals. It works at frightening speed, shifting, morphing and reorienting in every other moment, becoming difficult to pin down. Perceptiveness and awareness are our most valuable tools for reining in these tendencies. They allow us to identify the greedy and irrational side of our egos, see our own faults clearly and determine to change for the better.

It is a widely held belief that self-nature is innate. We allow it to be our default guide through the world, even if on occasion we act selflessly. Of course, it is in our hands to nurture selflessness instead of self-centredness. If we manage to do so from an early age, we can cultivate the kind-heartedness, friendliness, compassion and love deep within our young spirit. We can train our nature of non-self to leap into action whenever selfish intent arises and try to stop it before it manifests. This tug of war between selfishness and selflessness is part of what it means to be human.

Dharmic teachings are designed to help us cleanse ourselves of our self and embody our non-self. Non-self is the essential nature of the myriad phenomena, humans included. The teachings show us how the more ego- and self-driven we are, the greater our suffering through life becomes, while the more selfless we are, the freer, lighter and more at ease we feel. Living in the moment, perceiving and realising our mind-nature, these are the core tenets of Chan Buddhism and of the Buddhist cultivation practice. Even a momentary alignment with our non-self can reveal to us the true meaning and value of life.

CHAPTER FIVE

Manifestations of the Mind

Buddhist Dharma teaches us that every thought a person has, every word they speak and every action they perform are products of their mind-nature; their joy, their suffering, their lethargy – these, too, derive from their mind-nature. The quality of a person's nature of mind determines the quality of their life. Everything is a manifestation of the mind; the mind manifests everything.

Astronomers have shown the universe to be of an almost unimaginable size. Containing approximately a trillion Earth-like planets, the universe is estimated to stretch 1,560 billion light years across. It is perhaps surprising, then, that Earth remains the only place in the universe known to support life. How, between these trillion or so planets, is there not one tree or little critter? We are so lucky that this planet exists, that it is the way it is, and that humankind ended up on it.

Humans have so far named more than two million of the species that share this planet with us, with there probably being thousands, if not millions, of other species waiting to be discovered. Yet, it is we humans who possess the greatest wisdom and lifeforce of them all. Therefore, the onus is on us to show our appreciation and gratitude for the fortune that has been handed to us by nature – we should cherish this planet and the chance to live here. To that end, we must learn about ourselves and our place in the universe; the better we can do that, the better we will know how to express our thanks to Earth and our love for ourselves.

Buddhist Dharma teaches us that everything is the result of causes and conditions in flux. No worldly phenomenon exists in stasis, everything is in a constant state of change. Within the scope of human perception, nothing changes more quickly than our own thinking. Our thoughts change faster than the speed of light. And like our thoughts, it is a fact that all of our perceptions and sensations derive from our mind. Our mind is the source of everything. Huineng, the Sixth Patriarch of Chan, once said,

"The mind is the ground, and the mind-nature is the ruler who dwells on that ground…" It is a central belief of Buddhism that everything results from the mind. So, the nature of a person's mind determines how the world around them manifests to them and thus what kind of life they will have. But which nature of mind really rules the roost? The one driven by the self or the one guided by the non-self? Again, this is a matter of causes and conditions. If we want to kickstart changing our lives for the better, we must dedicate time to getting to know our mind-nature.

Everything is a manifestation of the mind. Specifically, it is a manifestation of the mind-nature. This means that the apparent characteristics we perceive as belonging to things are not true characteristics, they are simply creations of our mind. So, when different people look at the same thing, their responses differ. They experience sensations and instinctive responses that are unique to them, because each of them perceives a different thing, as manifested by their individual minds. Tellingly, these manifestations are determined by the quality of our mind-nature in the moment, which means if what we perceive is peaceful or chaotic, friendly or hostile, then such is the state of our mind-nature at that time.

Buddhist Dharma roughly divides manifestations of mind-nature into two groups: manifestations of the self-nature of mind and manifestations of the non-self nature of mind. Everything we perceive in this world is either a product of our self-mind or non-self mind. When our self-mind has primacy, our view of the world around us is marred by preconceptions. We approach the world in the way Bodhidharma warned of, "Understanding the world as we see it, and thereby understanding nothing." Non-self, on the other hand, is the essence of the myriad phenomena. When we navigate through the world from a place of non-self, we see everything with an open mind, we have no expectations. Like Bodhidharma put it, "To see without attachment is to see everything."

When the self-nature of mind has dominance, the world we manifest around us tends toward the self-centred and selfish.

We are more likely to appear tense, have a knitted brow, feel emotionally afflicted, uneasy or even enraged. But it is not only ourselves for whom these self-centred manifestations create affliction and suffering. Those around us can also suffer as a result. By contrast, when it is our non-self nature of mind that is manifest within us, we will appear calm and composed, an open, welcoming expression on our faces, and a feeling of ease and tranquillity underneath. Perhaps more importantly, we will provide comfort to those around us. So our every expression and gesture is a window into our state of mind-nature.

Everything arises from causes and conditions. Mind-nature is no exception. And just as other phenomena change as a result of changes in causes and conditions, so too do our mind-nature and its manifestations – of course, these things and manifestations and our mindset are all, in essence, one and the same – and since mind-nature changes as causes and conditions change, the possibilities of what it could manifest are limitless. So, the better we understand our mind-nature, the better equipped we will be to make choices about how to act and how to take control of our life. Buddhist Dharma can provide us with all the tools to achieve just that.

Human civilisation has a history of several thousand years. The chapters of that history have, in different regions, seen diverse events and stories unfold. In every corner of the occupied world, there have been times of peace and flourishing and times of chaos and war. But whatever happens to us, regardless of where we find ourselves and in what era, the human mind always remains king. History and experience teach us, for example, that lavish feasts with tables piled high with food do not bring lasting happiness; modest meals can be a cause for just as much joy. The state of the world is, of course, an important factor in the quality of our lives, but even more important in determining how we view our situation is our mindset. The universe, and the world for that matter, is vast, as is the amount of information they contain. We do not have room in our minds for everything that happens in the world. So our world consists of our realm of perception and awareness. Everything beyond that, everything someone else perceives but we don't, well, that is their world. They live in their world, you in yours, me in mine, and our worlds are different, but they also overlap. It is likely that even those parts of our lives that overlap appear differently for each of us, since we all make judgements of the external world and its phenomena according to our own value systems. We decipher our environment and experiences with our mind; our mind's manifestations represent everything for us.

Quality of life is something we in mundane society typically assess according to the material wealth a person has, whereas Dharma teaches us that everything about a person, their thoughts, perceptions, views, language and behaviour, derives from their mind-nature – their happiness and suffering included. The quality of our mental state and outlook thus determine the quality of our lives. This is why people can have entirely different feelings about the same thing. Some people will think it boring or painful. Others will feel happy because of it. These emotional responses are manifestations of mind-nature. So to be in control of our mental state is to be the master of our fate.

The meaning of life, according to Buddhist Dharma, lies in taking the wheel and steering ourselves away from suffering toward liberation. The key to achieving this is awakening to the essential nature of the mind, but we must first rid ourselves of the delusional ideas our "self" produces and free ourselves from its corrupting influence. Why is that? Buddhism tells us that the essential nature of everything is emptiness, an emptiness inherent to non-self. When we live our lives according to the whims of the "self" or ego, we are headed down a path counter to the essential nature of things, one which promises inevitable affliction and suffering. The source of all suffering is the self-nature of mind; that includes our suffering and that of everyone around us. Below is a brief look at how the self-nature of mind can manifest in our lives.

The most prominent characteristic of a manifest self-nature of mind is self-centredness, the idea that everything centres around us and around our own interests and feelings. At the core of self-centredness is the pursuit of maximising personal gain. Thinking to this end, when indulged, easily spirals and can quickly become unmanageable and seemingly all-consuming, even when we already have more than enough wealth and resources. Even with enough money to last a lifetime, or even ten lifetimes or more, the self is never satisfied. It always searches for more. Its desire knows no bounds.

As far as the self is concerned, the best approaches to maximising our personal gain are self-centredness and multitasking – or trying mentally to juggle as many matters as possible at once. Combined, these can only lead to "dualist, differentiating thought" and "attachments". It is fair to say that "desirousness" and "attachments" are the biggest indications of the self at work.

Desire, here, refers to wanting the "good things" in life – money, sex, fame, food, sleep. The self clings to these things. It pursues them and thinks up every way possible of getting more. The more they fill our life, the more satisfied our self appears to be. Desire drives the self, and desire is supreme. Everything else falls by the wayside. The self has no interest in our essential nature of non-self.

"Multitasking" is one of the self's favourite but most harmful habits. Without us noticing, it often devolves into chaotic thinking. The self drags our attention here, there and everywhere, diving it between multiple topics and subjects almost at once. While we're out and about, at home or at work, no matter what we're doing, our self has control of our thoughts. What about the stocks today, that upcoming mortgage payment, a chore left undone, family problems, friends missed, it could be anything… we will be busy with something and our mind will be chattering away about everything other than the task at hand – "my this", "my that", "my everything". Regret, nostalgia and focusing on the past, in particular, are some of the self's favourite weapons.

Desperate at all times to maximise personal interest, the self is never settled. Even when busy with something, the self will be distracted, its attention split, and its focus wandering far from the present moment. ◄◄

The self's motivation to reflect on past actions is cunning. Its goal is to work out how it might better scheme and direct us in the future to improve personal gain. Either way, whether it be lost in reflection on the past or making preparations for the future, the self refuses to remain in the present. It is at its most uncomfortable in the present; even when we are busy with something, it is always trying to split off and put as much distance as possible between us and now.

Manifestations of the self are myriad and ever-changing, they are elusive and difficult to pin down, but they never veer far from their essential purpose. Every one of them derives from an idea about the self as central to the universe. The self is equal parts intelligent and stupid. It knows how to lead our thinking astray, on long meandering treks through the past and future, to a point from which we struggle to return to our true selves. It lures us down dead ends and loses us in slumberous states. In fact, ever more people are dragging their feet through life in a kind of half-slumber. Looking at their phone while holding their child's hand to cross a road. Driving with their eyes on their screen. Walking with their heads down, scrolling. Eating and texting. We spend so much of our time not really paying attention to what we're doing, not to caring for our child, not to driving, not to walking, not to eating. It shows just how much the mind is enslaved to the ego.

Indeed, technological development is not always our ally. As our mobile phones become able to fulfil ever more tasks, their grip on our individual worlds becomes ever tighter. Now, our thoughts are led in the direction of whatever information pops up on our phones, putting us in mind of anything but the present moment. We are constantly jumping from role to role – reader of an article, watcher of a video, commentor on a social media post, daydreamer as we imagine ourselves as the character on our screens. The constant changes of self and of the world inside our phones overlap and pile up, producing in us an indescribably painful and confused emotional state. Many among us have sunk into the world of their phones beyond the point where they can save themselves. It is a state of being in which they never experience the present moment. They miss important sights and sounds. They neglect doing what they should. They are sleeping through their lives, mere shadows of themselves. For mundane society it is enough to open our eyes and set the brain turning for us to be deemed awake. However, Buddhism knows that what is more important is the contents of the mind.

The slumberous state in which many spend their lives is characterised by absence – by not being present. Not when we're driving, not when we're studying, not while at work. We eat, sleep, watch TV, go about our day – we make our way through life with our eyes open, but nobody home behind them. Though that might be a little harsh, since our eyes are open. But whatever negligible focus we have is threadlike, prone to breaking at any moment, at the slightest distraction. There is little difference between how present we are then and how present we are during sleep. To be awake, on the other hand, is as Dharma tells us a state of being self-aware and perceptive of one's surroundings in every moment. It is quite normal for us to live somewhere between these states of mind, present one moment, distracted the next. However, with the self still guiding us through life, our thoughts remain disordered, and we struggle to embody our nature of non-self. You have probably guessed that we should not settle for this state, it should not be our goal in life. Our aim should be to live in the present moment and to achieve abiding awareness.

The state of slumber described above is equivalent to having a dormant Buddha-nature, or non-self nature. Stripping us of awareness, it leaves behind only a constant stream of self-centred thought which nourishes the self-nature of mind. As a result, our mind becomes heavy and numb; it slowly closes up. We become insensitive to the things happening around us, to the people in our lives, to anyone, in fact, their pain and suffering, of which we ourselves might well be the cause, going unnoticed and even ignored. We develop a cold, unfeeling heart of stone and become bent on gaining profit by whatever means possible. In short, it is a state in which our rationality readily fails us, in which profit stands above all, and in which no consequence is too great in pursuit of it.

Life is precious. Sleeping through it would be a shame. It is there to be lived, with freedom and awareness – how beautiful a life that would be! Freedom, especially mental freedom, is the key to living a meaningful life. Most people have never broken the law and have lots of freedom to act as they wish, and more importantly than that, most people have complete freedom for their mind to go wherever they please. But, if we stop and pay attention for a moment, we will likely realise that our thoughts and our mind are in thrall to our self-nature of mind. We are under the self's control; its desires, feelings and perspectives lead us and our thoughts wherever they wish. We have lost our connection with that most primal part of us, our essential nature of non-self, and in the process, we have fallen out of touch with our conscience and kind-heartedness and have, in the pursuit of own selfish interests, started to cause harm to others through our actions.

Hurting others becomes a habit when we pass our lives in slumber. When our Buddha-nature is dormant, we only have our ego to guide us, which obfuscates our innate nature of non-self. Self-centredness ingrains in us a default attitude of antagonism and resistance to the people around us, which in turn severs our mind's connection to collective existence and our link to the present moment. Our mind becomes shackled by the desires of our ego, limiting our body and our actions. We lose control.

The mind is king. Everything is a manifestation of the mind. Happiness, suffering, ennui, freedom – these are all manifestations of the mind. Suffering, in particular, is a state of being divorced from the true essence of the universe. It derives from misjudgement and misunderstanding about our world and life, specifically, from an erroneous assessment that there exist such things as "permanence" and "self". Dharma teaches us that persistent belief in "permanence" and "self" blinds us to the essential nature of the myriad things. It produces in us a state of ignorance and slumber, in which afflictions and suffering are the norm. "Impermanence" and "non-self" characterise the essential nature of the myriad things. We must centre our view of the universe around them both in order to awaken to the true meaning of life and break free from our slumber and suffering.

The core aim of the self is to maximise personal gain; the default disposition of non-self is to abide by collective existence and align with the present moment. For non-self, everything that belongs to collective existence and personal gain of any kind is unimportant. For me, the Shenzhen singer Cong Fei represents one of the most unforgettable examples of non-self in action. His fee for a single performance in the 90s in Shenzhen was around ten thousand yuan, which meant that he could easily enough have enjoyed a life of luxury. But besides his music, Cong Fei dedicated much of his time to the Shenzhen Voluntary Union and, over a decade, he donated three million yuan of his savings to help children from impoverished families in the countryside, while he himself led a relatively spartan existence. When, at thirty-seven, he was diagnosed with late-stage stomach cancer, he did not have enough money to pay for treatment. But rather than complain, accepted his fate and faced it calmly. Before his death, he even changed his will to state that his corneas should be donated to medicine. They were eventually used to restore the sight of five people.

In his short life, Cong Fei channelled his resources into funding education for hundreds of children. He gave of himself entirely and displayed a truly embodied nature of non-self. His life is worth remembering: a life inverse to one driven by the self. Its opposite is a life of greed, parsimony, unscrupulousness and amorality; it is someone who is happy to harm others for personal benefit, for whom wealth is life's focus, to the extent that they would not part with a hair on their body to help another, not even their loved ones, not even if they are already rich.

Selfishness and egotism may bring short-lasting happiness, but inevitably they lead to an attitude of antagonism and resistance toward the people around you. The self always has an objective, an ulterior motive, in every matter big and small. When the self is in control, even something as everyday as eating is driven by some selfish intent. The self fosters expectations and attachments. It wastes our energy and attention on weighing up every possibility of a matter, even though, deep down, it is fully aware that a degree of uncertainty is unavoidable. The result is obvious. Before we act or have even made a decision, we have already exerted most of our stores of energy unnecessarily, worsening our physical and mental state and wearing our patience thin for any form of resistance. Anxiety, irritability, disappointment, fear and pain are among the negative emotions that could quickly follow. We receive countless lessons over the course of our lives that tell us how increased selfishness and egotism lead to loneliness and suffering. But often, we assimilate the lesson too late. So be attentive and consciously make efforts to be less self-centred; lower your expectations and relinquish your attachments. You might be surprised how soon you start to feel more relaxed and how much more energy you have all of a sudden.

It is our habit to centre our life around ourselves. This is due to the influence of our self-nature of mind. It focusses on selfish interests, attachments and expectations, leaving our emotions susceptible to the sway of external circumstances and environments. When things are going counter to our expectations, the ground quickly falls away from beneath us and we tumble into a bottomless pit of despair. Suffering, affliction, chaotic thinking and uncontrolled emotions all result from an uninhibited self. If we want a life free of such worries, we must align ourselves with the essential nature of myriad things – non-self.

Whether you have children or not, you are likely to have observed in the youth around you a certain characteristic. They are self-centred. Every choice they make is laced with a potent dose of self-interest. They expect and rely upon you to drive them to buy toys, take them to the swimming pool, give them their phone to play on, buy snacks for them and bring home McDonalds and KFC. When you say no, frustration quickly kicks in, and sometimes a temper tantrum follows, sometimes the waterworks begin.

Expectation and dependency are common among humans. But very few people are clear on a simple fact which might change their tendency toward them. That external causes and conditions are unreliable. This is why so much of what we expect and depend on in life comes to nothing or falls through or never materialises. Our usual reaction to such results is to suffer. We hurt, we worry, we curse our luck; we become anxious, afraid, frustrated. If a child grows up never learning not to put so much stock by their expectations and dependence, the life and work ahead of them promise even greater suffering. Education needs to begin at childhood about the dangers of expectation and dependency. While young, we should be allowed to experience some of the pain they bring, as this is crucial to encouraging us to make changes as we grow up. But there comes a point when we must embrace what the Buddha taught: do not look to the external, everything out there is a manifestation of the mind. The mind is what is most precious. If we must pursue something, must rely on and have expectations of something, make it mental cultivation. Don't look to the external world for anything. External causes and conditions are beyond our control; what we can control is our inner mind. Liberation awaits in the absence of hopes and demands.

There are two sides to everything. There is no absolute good or absolute bad. Self-centredness, or rather self-interest, has its own kind of logic as a worldly method of survival of the individual. Naturally, individuality and self-interest must have value, since the universe bestowed humankind with them. Similarly, self-nature of mind has its merits. It can be beneficial to maximise personal gain, to be unsatisfied with everything, to stimulate our desire to improve our skills and to compete. Our self is adept at adapting in order to survive under society's pressures and our everchanging environment. It is thanks to the self that we can learn flexibility, how to strive harder and how to increase our efficiency. We are able to invent new technologies for the service of humankind because of the influence of the self. These are all manifestations of our self-nature of mind striving to improve.

Many very talented people – high achieving students, authors, artists, sociologists, economists, computer scientists and successful businesspeople, all of whom contribute to society – would not achieve their potential without a drive to better themselves and work hard. There is no doubt that the fighting spirit inherent in the self has played an indispensable role in society's economic development and flourishing. So, we must concede that, according to the relative view of things, self-nature of mind is an innate aspect of the individual's mind, without which humankind might not be the humankind we know today, we might not be where we are now as a race, and the world would likely be a very different place. Everything is, of course, the result of causes and conditions, the majority of which lie beyond human control. All we can do as individuals is to work to improve ourselves and grow, in the hope of changing our fate.

Without our willing it or even being aware of it happening, how our mind-nature is manifest at any one moment changes in accordance with causes and conditions. Under certain conditions, our self-nature of mind will wholly manifest, giving full reign to our most egotistical and self-centred aspects. We might ignore our loved ones or colleagues or pressure them into following our will. In other conditions, our non-self nature of mind will arise, bringing to the fore our selflessness, our need to help others and to give of ourselves. We will radiate warmth and happiness to all people around us. We all have two sides, and we can decide which one we nurture most. Embodying our non-self has its challenges, especially in today's society. It requires that we be conscious of our every word and action, that we shine the light of awareness on our inner being. This is how to purify ourselves of the self-nature's influence over us and to give space for our essential nature of non-self to manifest.

Non-self nature of mind revolves around collective existence. It centres on the present moment. It fosters kind-heartedness, modesty and a love for helping others. Self-nature of mind is self-centred. Its core focus is maximising personal gain at any cost and will harm others to do so. It often disguises its true intentions and has a knack for glossing over and twisting all things that others see as negative. Greed is what drives it, but it will often pretend magnanimity. On the inside, the self-driven person is drooling with envy but puts on a front of disinterest. They are seething beneath their calm exterior. In order to achieve their goals, they will think up every way of hiding their intent from others. The self-nature of mind keeps its thoughts hidden. Its hectic, mercurial thinking is hard to fathom. It is deliberate and conniving and difficult to perceive. The intent of a self-driven person easily evades our notice.

Old Path White Clouds speaks to this aspect of the self. One afternoon, when the Buddha met King Pasenadi, seven ascetic monks happened to pass by. Pasenadi went over to greet them, then returned to the Buddha's side and asked: "Lord, according to you, have any of those ascetics yet attained Arhatship? Are any of them close to attaining such fruits?"

The Buddha answered, "Your majesty, you live the life of a ruler and thus are more accustomed to men of government and politics. It is only natural that you would find it difficult to ascertain which monks have attained certain levels of spiritual practice. But in fact, it is difficult for anyone to know whether or not someone is enlightened after merely meeting them once or twice. It is necessary to live close to them, observing them carefully to see how they respond to difficult circumstances, to see how they converse with others, and to understand the depth of their wisdom, virtue, and attainment."

It is a relative truth that individual self-nature of mind and collective non-self nature of mind are both essential aspects of humanhood which have been gifted to us by the universe. By bringing these two sides of our essential nature into harmony, we can find our true self. What that requires is dedication to embodying our inherent non-self and toning down our often-overactive self. "Realising one's nature is the path to Buddhahood, otherwise mundanity will be one's fate." Only by realising our nature of non-self can we begin to align with our true self. The longer we remain in touch with our non-self, the deeper the connection we can form with it, and the truer and more prolonged its manifestation.

There are many people who take exception to the idea that everything is a manifestation of the mind. They believe that the mind's influence over us and our world is negligible. But can that really be the case? It does not take much experience of the mind's significance in everything we do and perceive for us to realise that we should not underestimate it. In fact, every physical action and thought leaves a trace. Merely thinking about an action produces an indelible mark. If we have covetous thoughts, for example, when we see what other people possess, whether or not we act upon them, we have already created a change within ourselves, a subtle change perhaps, but one that strengthens and solidifies our harmful habits. Over time, what started out as a niggling thought might manifest as behaviour, which if allowed to continue could lead down a slippery slope.

Certain behaviours leave behind obvious trails, while others leave behind subtle ones. The latter tend to manifest in almost imperceptible ways, as if nothing has happened or changed. But outside our notice they consolidate a certain kind of mental disposition. For the benefit of laypeople wanting to purify themselves of these unwanted accumulations of character, the Buddha taught of the concepts of "karma", "karmic reward" and "meritorious virtue", helpful vocabulary for understanding many of the phenomena of causes and effect. Dharma explains that a person's motivation for their behaviour is incredibly important. The aim manifest in our mind as we take certain actions to a large extent determines the fruits we reap. Behaviour and thinking based in "selflessness and altruism" produce good karma, while "selfish and self-centred" thoughts and actions accumulate bad karma. In other words, whatever distances us from the self brings good karma and whatever strengthens our selfish habits brings bad karma; whatever moves us closer to non-self provides good karma and whatever takes us away from non-self provides bad karma. Cultivating "good karma" and "karmic rewards" is for many people the motivation for practising Buddhist Dharma.

Most of us live long lives, with decades ahead or behind us. Yet, the individual self seems always to feel pressed by a sense of urgency. The more selfish a person, the greater the fear they feel in the face of death. Experiencing their bodies gradually deteriorate, watching as the reputation, status, wealth and family they have worked tooth and nail to build over many years slowly slip from their fingertips, what chance is there that their self, their ego, will not shudder in fear? As death approaches, the self is gripped by terror at its helplessness. Non-self, however, is fearless. It knows that at its essence it is timeless. It is perpetual and constant. It has existed since before the beginning of the universe.

Rather than disguising our own inner thoughts by controlling our expressions and behaviours, we must take responsibility for changing ourselves for the better by changing our inner selves. The goal of Buddhist cultivation is to awaken to the essential nature of the mind. Doing so will change us inside and out and will bring us freedom from suffering, but first it will rid us of selfishness and egotism and bring out our kind-heartedness, compassion and selflessness. On the path of cultivation, correcting our habits, be they physical or mental, is an essential daily practice. In curing ourselves of the corruption of the self, whatever method we use is correct, as long as our intent is true. Just as if, after walking for decades in one direction down a road, we realise we have been going the wrong way and only need to turn around to get back on track. No matter how we travel this path, as long as we take it in the right direction, we will reach our destination eventually.

A practitioner who has already established a connection with their nature will lead a life without attachments. They will go with the flow, embracing causes and conditions while, at the same time, like a lotus flower, rising above them. They will not be swept up by external changes, be led astray by material wealth or nurture their ego; they will live contentedly and peacefully in the present moment, taking every day and every instant as it comes and accepting the gifts of life as they present themselves. Such a person will soon realise the true meaning of life.

The goal of cultivating Buddhist Dharma is to realise the Buddha nature within us and embody our true selves. Once aligned with our true selves, we can work in any job, be it selling vegetables at the market or brokering real estate, be it as a housewife or a sociologist or an economist or a scientist, or even a successful businessperson, and like Vimalakīrti from the age of the Buddha, lead a life full of wisdom and compassion.

CHAPTER SIX

The Way to Dharmic Awareness

Awareness is a very important human quality. A rare and fleeting quality, it is the tool we use to exchange addictions for purposeful habits, rein in our wayward thinking and settle in the present moment, to transform afflictions into bodhi wisdom, replace selfishness with selflessness and break free of our deluded notions of 'permanence' and 'self' in order to embrace an attitude of 'impermanence' and 'non-self'. Ultimately, awareness can bring us back to our true selves. There is no question that awareness is the path to liberation.

For the majority of us laypeople, the self-nature of mind threatens to take over at every moment, until we are consumed by ego. The Buddha laid out the path of awareness to guide us toward a reacquaintance with our natures of non-self, of finding our Buddha nature.

The Buddha was the first among humans to discuss awareness in a systematic manner. Even today, the most schematic, most grounded practices of awareness derive from the Buddha's teachings.

The everchanging and unpredictable phenomena of the world are the cause of much bewilderment and disorientation for most laypeople. We feel lost one moment and confused the next; frustrated, then distressed. To help lead us out of this state of being, the Buddha provided a guide guide – the Dharma – to identifying the truth of the universe and to awaken to the essential nature of our mind. The reason he gave for why we cannot see the true form of things is that we are too attached to the notion of there being 'impermanence' in the universe and a 'self' who experiences it. Such delusions only blind us to the essential nature of the universe.

Buddhist Dharma explains that there are two kinds of insight. One is provided by self. Dharma calls this view deluded, casting it as the source of all suffering. It is the default mode of our self-nature of mind. The other is guided by non-self, which Dharma refers to as the right view and the only guide on the path from suffering to liberation.

Why do these two forms of insight lead, respectively, to and away from suffering? Because self and non-self are two distinct modes of cognition. If our basepoint for all cognition is self, we very quickly begin to think it normal to view and move through the world in a self-centred way. If, on the other hand, we process the world in the firm knowledge that no such thing as the self exists, we have more chance of prioritising the collective existence over our own and it is easier for us to embody our nature of non-self and embrace the flux of every moment.

In all honesty, this is not an easy state of being to achieve and maintain. Even if persistent reminders about the non-existence of self often do not suffice to hold off the ego's influence. Our best hope of success is to begin by working at selflessness in one area of our lives at a time, breaking down the task of transforming our habits into manageable chunks, all the while ensuring that we remain clear on the right view of things. Start on the right path and start small, that is the road to success.

Hopefully, the power of the right view is clear. One invaluable tool for harnessing it is awareness.

Why is awareness so important? And how does it relate to the universal principle discovered by the Buddha?

Typically, over the trajectory of their arising to abiding to ceasing to be, phenomena develop powerful predispositions. Humans, for example, continuously consolidate our notion of self long into our lives, cementing its position as our default mode of cognition. Even occasional moments of clarity, in which we realise the harm our ego is causing us and the people around us, glimpse the truth of things and embody non-self, are not enough to break the hold the self has over us, not if we do not work to foster awareness and never stop.

Specifically, we need to cultivate an awareness of when the 'self' surfaces in our day to day. When 'I' am, when 'I' think, when 'I' feel, when 'I' do, we must pay attention. The unchecked self is the source of all suffering. We must first notice it if we hope to rid ourselves of its influence and of deluded thinking. Whenever the 'self' arises, it blinds us from the true nature of things. Awareness is thus the key to cleansing ourselves of self-centred habits and thinking, and to switching our default mode of cognition to the right view. Like a CCTV camera, we must aim our awareness to monitor our every action and thought for the presence of our ego, leaving it nowhere to hide.

Most of the time our attention is split and unfocused. Our train of thought roves here and there without rhyme or reason. This is the fault of an overbearing sense of self. As the self tries to find a means of maximising personal gain in everything we do, it spreads our thinking thin, searching for opportunity down multiple paths at once, leading us to try and juggle two or even more matters at once. This is the reason why so many of us watch TV while we eat or browse our phones while we have a conversation with a person sitting next to us. Whatever sliver of attention is left over will be put scheming how to manipulate people and things to derive the greatest benefit. The self pulls our thoughts away from the present and lives in the clouds.

Here is one common example of how the self leads our thinking astray. Imagine you have investments in the stock market. Every day, the moment you wake up, you turn on your phone and read the financial news, note whether Dow Jones Industrial Average is on the up or down, check if there are any developments specific to your investments. As you do this, you are probably brushing your teeth, getting dressed, eating breakfast or taking the children to school, and you continue this multitasking right up to nine fifteen when the stock market starts trading. From then on, your day is even more dominated by thoughts of 'my stocks', all the time you are at work, eating lunch, going on break and headed home. It is constant.

As your stocks fluctuate, so do your thoughts and emotions. Excitement or dismay follows every change. Whether you are in a meeting, talking to clients, reading a document or with your children, your mind is elsewhere. You are indifferent to anything happening around you. Walking along the street, your attention on your phone watching for updates, you might step in dog poo, bump into other pedestrians or walk out in front of a car. You probably trip every hundred meters, but hardly notice. Nothing else in the world is as important as your stocks. You spend the day never being present, and it is not like the stock market is going to close anytime soon. It will stay open until you're seventy or eighty years old, by which time, if your stocks remain the focus of your days, just think how much time you will have wasted. No amount of money you earn can replace that. All of those days behind you with nothing of significance to remember them by. You have sacrificed that most precious of things – presence.

Everything we know in our lives is the result of a harmony of causes and conditions. Harmony is what gives our lives meaning; gives this moment meaning. It imbues the present with significance. The goal of awareness is to observe whether we are in harmony with the present moment or whether the self has taken over. *Old Path White Clouds* explains that the Buddha believed that the only way to reconnect with life and our true selves was to return to the present moment. The stronger our ego, the Dharma teaches, the more self-centred and chaotic our thinking becomes. Awareness is the only way back to our true self.

Now that we know this, the hard work begins. Simply deciding to be aware does not guarantee success. A few seconds, a minute, or even a couple of minutes of awareness here and there, do not amount to true presence. Maintaining that state for long, full periods of time is what is required. As far as I understand, the self-nature of mind is the prime culprit for pulling us away from the present moment. The greater the control our self has over us, the more easily our attention becomes distracted and divided, dragging our mental state ever further away from the present. When we feel our thoughts start to rove, it is our responsibility to switch on our awareness and get the self in our crosshairs.

The world we live in and navigate through exists as the result of causes and conditions. It is a trait unique to non-self to have the awareness to embrace these causes and conditions as they shift and change and our apparent reality shifts and changes too. Conversely, the self believes that its will is king. It overestimates its power to control the moment, trying to replace the actual present conditions for what it believes will be better for itself. Doing so disconnects us from the now. The way back to the present is through reconnecting with our non-self and relinquishing the self's control and need to be at the centre of things.

What does embracing present causes and conditions look like? There is a classic story about the Buddha we can look to for a hint. One day, while instructing his followers in the Dharma, the Buddha picked up a lotus flower. The audience waited for him to speak, but he never did. They looked on, not understanding why he had plucked the flower from the water. Only the disciple Mahākāśyapa, seeing the Buddha take the flower, smiled. Immediately, the Buddha smiled back at him and said aloud, 'I possess the true Dharma eye, the marvellous mind of Nirvana, the true form of the formless, the subtle [D]harma [G]ate that does not rest on words or letters but is a special transmission outside of the scriptures. This I entrust to Mahākāśyapa.'[3] The Buddha then

_____

3
   Heinrich Dumoulin (2005). Zen Buddhism: A History. p. 9

explained to his disciples why he had picked the flower. He said that in this moment, the flower embodies the wondrous true form, a fact that his disciples failed to perceive because of the interference of their thoughts. Mahākāśyapa connected with the flower in the present moment, this is why he smiled. The flower only showed its true form to the disciple who was living in the present moment. For the rest, the lotus was meaningless.

Life is at its best – at its most valuable – when we take a firm hold of the present, when we immerse ourselves in the universe before our eyes, when we live in sync with the moment happening now, and now, and now. The Buddha said that only with awareness can we find beauty in life and harmonise with the present. Awareness calms the mind; it provides conscious focus on a single thing at any one time. We can foster it by carefully chewing and tasting every mouthful of food, by feeling every step as we walk, by listening attentively to every word a friend or colleague is saying to us, and replying with all of our attention on the words we choose and utter, saying goodbye and shaking hands in a fully present mindset when we wish them goodbye. Concentrate on only one thing at any one time, whether that be talking, walking, sitting, lying down, eating, drinking or dressing. That, and that alone, is living in the present moment.

However, as far as I understand it, in order to achieve this state of being, it is necessary to first manifest the nature of non-self within us. To this end, we must come to terms with our relationship as individuals to the collective, and consequently give ourselves to collective existence, in terms of both respect and service. The individual who serves and follows the collective has embodied their essential nature of non-self; in a sense, they have embraced their role as a drop of water within the ocean. An individual that does not serve the collective either has a swollen idea of their own importance and believes they have no time for the collective, or they have never considered the existence of the collective and cannot therefore imagine how they might fit into it. If we do not have a clear understanding of the concept of collective existence, we cannot begin to foster respect for it, let alone serve it. Without a doubt, recognising and having reverence for the collective gives a better chance of dethroning the self.

The universe is the largest manifestation of collective existence that there is. To explain, anything that represents a collection of individual sentient beings and phenomena can be called a collective. Collective is a relative concept, set in opposition to the individual. In a family, it might the living members and everyone else in the ancestral tree combined that represent the collective; in a household, the parents, children, and perhaps grandparents, together represent a collective. Of course, it is the elder members of a family who most commonly have authority, and the younger generation respects and, perhaps even occasionally, serves them; this is how as children we learn humility and politeness, gaining the skills to better manage future relationships, be they professional or social. But the elder members of the family also serve the younger ones, and in doing so they learn much about themselves and their place in the collective family. If we understand our role in our family and strive to fill it well, then we already know what it is to be an individual within a collective.

It is a great shame that there are many younger people nowadays who do not respect the elders in their family, nor understand how to and why they should. This boils down to a refusal to participate in the collective; it is a mark of self-centredness, which signals selfish behaviour ahead. Worryingly, this kind of attitude only consolidates over the years it is left unchecked, and readily seeps into professional and social life. Whether beside a boss, colleague, friend, relative or spouse, the self-centred individual always regards themself as more important. It is life path certain to lead to constant rejection and rebuff, and inescapable antagonism and suffering. The life experiences of countless others provide us with cast-iron proof that the more selfish and egotistical you are, the worse you suffer. So, do not underestimate the power of a child's attitude toward their elders in determining their future—it represents their attitude to the collective.

Foster awareness of the self, of your thoughts and of presence;

be aware of what collective existence is and how to give respect and service to it. One precedes the other, yet each complements the other. Awareness is key to gaining a good handle of the self and of the collective and our individual place within it. It is the first step to embodying non-self.

In a sense, the 'present moment' is another kind of collective existence. By tuning into it, we are tuning into the natural, true state of things. We are giving ourselves over to something bigger than ourselves. Therefore, living in the present is a state of non-self, and the longer an individual can maintain presence, the more fully in alignment they are with their nature of non-self and with their true self.

Living in the present moment is an aspect of Buddhist practice. The 84,000 practices of Buddhist Dharma all require that we the practitioners remain in the present moment as much as possible throughout our self-cultivation, as this signifies a deep connection with collective existence, and alignment with present causes and conditions.

It is a fact that every one of us has at some point experienced being in the present moment. The reason why we do not experience the state more often is that the self has a powerful inclination toward differentiation and discrimination. It deems the present moment unimportant relative to the many means of maximising its interests that it imagines are out there waiting to be capitalise on. The stubborn habits of split attention and multitasking, once formed, are difficult to break. They readily become our fixed mode of operation if not brought under control, such that no matter how important the matter at hand, we are unable to bring ourselves into the present in order to pay it the attention it requires.

A differentiating mind disregards any present moment that it does not consider pressing, and pays attention only when it sees fit. Like a frog in a saucepan who thinks nothing of its situation when the water is tepid and only reacts when it senses the temperature rise past a certain point, by which time it is already too late, we often approach life in a similar way. This is the fault of our lacking awareness and not living in the present moment.

Buddhist Dharma places great emphasis on the present moment. Chan Buddhism, especially, advocates no-thought and accepting origination. Origination is a dependent process, Dharma explains. When the conditions for future origination have not yet aligned, there is no amount of human power that can control them. So the future is full of unknowns. Regardless how long we live, the past will always be the past and the future will remain in the future. Tomorrow promises uncertainty; the future beyond that even more so. Certainty exists only in the present moment. Our lives are a chain of such moments of certainty, and if only we can be present during these moments can we reap the benefits of living life in its truest form. Life is short and extremely precious. Yet the self is set on pursuing future benefits and realising desires, exhausting our mental energy through multitasking and planning, and frittering away our valuable time. This is the default setting of the self.

It is the exact opposite mode to that of a mind centred on emptiness and non-self, a mind for which life's value always lies in the now; for which the length of life is inconsequential and quality is what counts. Being at ease in the present moment promises a better life than whatever it is that internal desires and external materiality might appear to offer. The highest realm of life, Buddhist Dharma tells us, is life lived in the present moment and centred around emptiness and the collective.

The first job for a new practitioner, then, is to cultivate an awareness of the self and its modes of operation, and to become aware of how frequently they are truly present. Shining the light of awareness on the self is the only way of weaking its hold over us. When we finally break free, our non-self can rise to the fore, and our thoughts will naturally return to the now.

Another thing we must turn our awareness to is our emotions

Our emotions are also inextricably linked to the self, to the extent that we could say all emotions derive from the self. For this reason, our emotional state is sensitive to external influence. When people act or something unfolds counter to how we hope, it lights the fuse for an emotional outburst. If we do not have the awareness to catch ourselves before we blow, then the chances of us reeling ourselves back in once we do are minimal. Something as simple as this, if we are not careful, can send us and our lives into a spiral. Awareness of our emotions requires conscious effort. But we can also observe our emotions as a passer-by does something happening in the street. When we feel unhappy, we should observe the reason. When we are angry, we look for the cause. Slowly, we will realise that every one of our emotions comes from the self.

Bodhidharma wrote in the Dharma Methods of Pacifying the Mind: 'The self is ego. A fully realised being, on encountering some difficulty, does not despair, and on feeling fortune's favour, does not rejoice, because they have no self to speak of.' The source of all sentient beings' emotions is ego – the self. The core of awareness is to observe this 'self', the emotions it produces and the behaviour it leads to. As our awareness deepens, our ability to monitor our emotions improves, giving us the chance to work consistently on the bad habits and unwanted tendencies our self has nurtured. Eventually, we will have 'no self to speak of' either, and can fully realise our essential nature.

We must also turn our awareness to the deeper aspects of ourselves and our understanding of the world around us. The Buddha taught that awareness is understanding, and the path to understanding is the path to liberation. Understanding can help us to recognise the true form of phenomena. Understanding can provide wisdom and rid us of suffering. Understanding, as the Buddha described it, must be divorced from the self. It requires conscious effort and the lens of non-self. So, in order to achieve true understanding of the essence of all things, we must first cultivate a state of non-self.

Relationships supported by fragile emotional bonds are characterised by frequent misunderstandings. The self is, again, the cause both this emotional fragility and the inability to navigate around it. The self refuses to cultivate mutual understanding, empathy and trust, without which broken expectations drive emotions high and disagreements follow. When this happens, some people might block the other person on a social network, or simply break ties with them entirely. Before we jump to conclusions, though, and do something we regret, it is important that we consider the other person – things might not have gone as they had planned, there could be some nuance they struggled to express, they did not want for whatever reason to explain themselves fully, or they did not have time to do so. This happens all the time and is easily resolvable, but we often let our emotions get in the way, sometimes bringing an end to a long-lasting relationship. It is a real shame.

Awareness and non-self are therefore key to our approach to understanding things in a way that will bring us closer to realising their essential nature, saving us from unnecessary suffering.

Seeing to the true nature of things is difficult for us because everyday society is rife with self-centredness. So, the true form of the self is even more elusive. The self is self-centred and obsessed with gain. Blinded to the afflictions and suffering resulting from its pursuits by any brief moment of happiness or success it apparently earns, the self renders us incapable of perceiving our true nature of non-self.

Non-self is a state free of attachment and expectations. A life lived according to the human nature of non-self is exactly opposite to the life created by the self. However, shifting gears is easier said than done. A self-centred person will struggle to embody the non-self within them. So, it is best that we begin sooner rather than later to cultivate awareness, it is a demanding endeavour that takes time and patience. How long it takes to cultivate quality awareness depends entirely on our individual capacity and origination.

Engaging in the practice of awareness is an essential daily

lesson for any practitioner, and one that can teach us many lessons. For one, awareness of our every action and word can help us learn how to stop our selfishness from harming others. One core tenet of Nikaya Buddhism is to avoid committing harm. Nikaya is commonly thought of as the foundation for Mahayana. Therefore, if you have not properly cultivated the teachings of Nikaya Buddhism, you cannot succeed as a student of Mahayana. Money and selfish interests, our words and our behaviour— they can all harm other people if we do not approach them with awareness. What's more, if we have awareness, we are in a position to notice and rectify any harm we might accidentally cause others.

The Buddha explained the power of awareness with the following analogy. If someone is angry at me, I can naturally respond with anger and fight fire with fire, except this approach will only worsen the suffering of everyone involved. If, instead, I approach the situation with awareness, try to understand what has happened and why the person is angry with me, all the while keeping calm, then finding a solution will be easy. If the reason is an error on our part, we only need take responsibility; if there has been some misunderstanding, we can try to locate the cause, and explain our true intent. By being understanding, we can be honest with each other, which is an effective means of averting interpersonal crises.

Antagonism and resistance are the self's favourite methods of self-preservation, even though they invariably bring suffering. Worst of all is when it is another person who suffers as a result of our attitude, since it breeds further antagonism and resistance, worsening any feelings of hate and suffering, and on, and on it goes. Awareness of our actions gives us the chance to transform into bodhi wisdom any affliction we feel we have suffered. Without awareness, our feelings of antagonism and resistance spiral until understanding becomes impossible.

Awareness is vital for the future of humankind. It is a rare, powerful quality that has transformative powers; it helps us rein in disordered thoughts, live in the present moment and create wisdom out of suffering. It lays the path away from selfishness and toward selflessness, away from notions of 'permanence' and 'self' and toward the right view. Ultimately, it brings us back to our true self. Awareness points the way to liberation.

In the fourth chapter, we looked at how we, as individuals, fit into collective existence, how individuals should respect and serve the collective, and how individuals should protect and live in harmony with one another. This is the way of nature in our universe.

The key to individuals maintaining such harmony is love. Actually, to love is both a method of cultivation and an eventual result of self-cultivation. Love refers to the active or conscious effort to satisfy the needs of someone for whom we have strong and deep feelings. To love oneself is not love, it is a manifestation of the self. Love centred on another person and that doesn't apply pressure are selfless forms of love – they are true love.

Love is the active or conscious effort to satisfy the needs of someone for whom we have strong and deep feelings. True love requires that we give of ourselves to others. It must be centred on other people without putting them under pressure. It must be selfless. ▶▶

Love is a constant feature of our lives, whether it be love shared with a single person or the combination of love felt in multiple relationships. If that love is highly selfish and high-pressure, then suffering is inevitable. A better quality of love is possible with awareness. But first we must understand love, which seems simple but is actually very complex. Generally, there are two kinds. One is based on the existence of a 'self' and happens between parents and children, other relatives and close friends. It is mixed up with attachments, differentiation and pressure. Recipients of this kind of love often feel restricted, tortured and hurt, and for that reason what was once love can readily devolve into resentment. This kind of love relies heavily on dualist, differentiating thinking—love for what one has, and dislike for other things.

'If the mind possesses notions of value, it must equally see some things as low; if the mind possesses a notion of right, it must equally have a notion of wrong.' (*Bodhidharma, The Treatise on the Two Entrances and Four Practices*). Differentiating love excludes people outside the inner circle or treats them with indifference. It is a love guided by the self's preconceived notions and often only exacerbates the suffering of ourselves and others.

The other kind of love is compassionate and empathetic love. Compassion is the capacity of the mind to bring others happiness; empathy is a drive to put oneself in others' shoes and relieve them of suffering. Compassionate and empathetic love is selfless. It does not differentiate and does not require reciprocation. Compassionate and empathetic love is love for everyone, not just those near to you.

For us laypeople, selfish habits run deep, so when we talk about love we are mostly referring to the kind that derives from our notion of self. Awareness is the answer to this love. It will help us see how selfish and self-centred this kind of love is, and put us on track to exchanging it for a more selfless kind. Awareness is the only tool with which we can restrain the self and thereby allow non-self to take over. Once we have embodied non-self, we can achieve true love.

Understanding requires awareness, the goal of which is to cleanse us of the 'self' and embody non-self. Understanding based in selfless intent is deeper than anything the self can provide, just as selfless love is more sincere than any love of the self. This reminds me of a time at friend's teahouse. My friend has a number of regulars come to drink tea and chat most days, each of them with a different background, which makes for interesting conversations and a sometimes heated atmosphere, since disagreements are common.

Once, one of the customers took a syringe out of his bag and went to the restroom. Suspicious, the rest of the clientele waited in suspense while he returned, to ask him what he was doing. He explained that he had developed diabetes, at only thirty years old, because he had spent his young adulthood working and socialising nonstop. That was twenty years ago at that point. For the first decade he had taken western oral medication and after that had switched to insulin, two shots daily. The other customers either looked guilty for having thought badly of him, or sympathetic for the turn his life had taken. In any case, that day their conversation involved none of the usual bickering, and whatever he said everyone else seemed to agree with. It was clear, from then on, that the others were trying to accommodate their friend, often offering to help him out. There was more care toward him than before. You see, understanding gives us a window into the truth of things. The better we understand something, the more we trust it, accept it and love it. The Buddha said that when you have understanding and love, success is guaranteed down all avenues.

Inversely, the less we understand, the more readily we make mistakes, and the more likely conflicts are to occur. The can only lead to antagonism and opposition. Between spouses, each of whom has their own ideas and plans, this kind of situation can be fatal for love; between parents and children and siblings, it means strained tolerance and no compromise or generosity; between friends, it makes for a relationship waiting to be dissolved at the first sign of contradiction. Sincere hope for the wellbeing of the people in our lives requires a foundation of awareness and understanding. Awareness and understanding of these people's suffering and expectations can help us realise how best to alleviate their pain and aid them towards their aspirations. This is true love. If we simply neglect their needs and expect them to follow our wishes, that is selfish love.

For every practitioner, awareness is a foundational quality that requires cultivation. Without it, we have no hope of success in our Buddhist practice. Cultivation requires rectifying our values and behaviours, and curing us of the influence of the self-nature of mind. Only daily awareness of the self, cultivated over decades, will strengthen our ability to keep track of how it intrudes into our life, and will provide us with the insights needed to make true progress. It is not hard to see that awareness of the self is core to our awareness practice – that means awareness of our thoughts, sensations and emotions, including love, and of how the self controls or features in them.

The self is with us at all times. It wields its influence on everything we do, every word we speak, every thought we have. Its reach is so extensive that we may at times feel incapable of deep awareness. From my experience, when we feel like this, an effective tactic is to apply awareness to what seem like matters of priority. If that is our relationships, then we should make an effort to identify the effects of the self on all of our relationships, whether that be our self or the self of others. If our relationships with our relatives, friends or colleagues is not good, it likely indicates that either we are very selfish, and they are choosing to avoid us, or they are very selfish, and we are choosing to avoid them.

When it comes to our relationship with our parents or with our children, things are simpler. Any problems are ours. They are all related to our own selfishness and egotism. Let's think back a moment through our own lives. Anyone who has children has at some point, driven by their selfish love for the child, allowed their child to be self-centred, and let their self-centredness grow within them. It is possible this happened at the expense of lots of other people, as long as their own child was given centre stage. It is no stretch of the imagination to suggest that these children will then have grown up self-centred, and will no doubt persist in their selfish tendencies for the foreseeable future, likely causing discomfort in others and drawing dislike from the people around them.

Origination is dependent; everything is the result of causes and conditions. Selfishness in children is no different; it is instilled in them by their parents. The relationship between parent and child is one of lead and follow. If a parent is self-centred, then will the child not follow their example? You reap what you sow. It is a parent's responsibility to trace any problematic behaviour back to its cause and observe how their child conducts themselves in the world. In doing so, a parent might observe echoes of their own character in their children's selfishness. Again, awareness is the answer. It is how we perceive the error of our self-centred ways and how we know to set to improving our relationship with our parents or our children or our friends or colleagues. It starts with the self, and it starts in the now.

My own experience tells me that a good place to begin our practice of awareness is from the idea that the more self-centred we are, the more we suffer. Think about it for a moment. When we are multitasking, being pulled in several directions at once, walking while looking at our phones, leading our child down the street while taking a call, just how many things could go wrong? We need to recognise every risk to our and our child's safety that multitasking creates. We might step into a pothole, get knocked down by a bike or step out in front of a car. But if we can catch ourselves in the middle of walking while browsing our phones and remind ourselves of the potential dangers it poses, we will be more likely to identify this version of the self's influence in the future.

Similarly, if we lose our temper when things don't go our own way and blow up at the people around us, we are embodying the archetype of the self-centred person. Our anger in this kind of situation creates tension and makes others feel uncomfortable. It also does nothing good for us. Neither does looking down on others, which is another manifestation of self-centredness. But in either situation, if we were to put ourselves in the other's shoes, we will likely get a taste of how they feel in response to our behaviour and attitude. Everybody is equal. Everybody has a self. Everyone hopes to have harmonious relationships with others. Selfishness and egotism can disrupt the balance, and negative emotions can quickly lead to antagonism and opposition, so that in the end, nobody wins. All it takes is awareness of our actions and the results they produce for us to know that we must change our behaviour and mindset in the future, for our own benefit and for the benefit of everyone else in our lives.

Another helpful awareness practice is to put our skill of awareness to the test to tackle more difficult areas of our disposition. Perhaps the hardest habits to cure ourselves of are the self's hypocritical tendencies and self-disguise. It is a common tactic of the self to feign selflessness and charity, kindness, love and generosity. So it is important to remember that external appearances often contradict what is really happening underneath.

Possibly the worst part about this illusion and misdirection is that it is not only others the self is fooling, but itself as well. Fooling others with a blend of truth and lies is bad enough; but fooling ourselves is worse. When we lose touch with truth and sincerity, life quickly loses its flavour, a situation we will struggle to resolve if we are not proactive practitioners of self-awareness. So, catch yourself in your own lies and hypocrisy, and watch your cultivation soar; manifesting your true nature of non-self is not far behind.

Awareness is the practice of identifying the damage caused by the self, the source of all of humankind's afflictions and suffering. Awareness is insight into this truth, the first step in dethroning the self and elevating non-self.

Every one of the Buddha's teachings requires that we experience the wisdom it contains for ourselves. Doing so is not possible without awareness. The purpose of awareness is to observe our self-driven actions and how those actions only cause harm. It shines the light on the truth that the source of all suffering is attachment to deluded views about the existence of 'permanence' and 'self'. We must embrace 'impermanence' and 'non-self' if we are to make our suffering disappear. The highest realm of awareness is attained through understanding the essential nature of the myriad things and the threat posed by the self. We must set an intention to leave self-centredness behind and to move forward with selfless love in our hearts, toward realignment with our essential nature of non-self.

CHAPTER SEVEN

The Law of Cause and Effect

The universe operates according to the law of cause and effect. It is a principle that dictates our lives and the trajectories of all phenomena of the mundane world. Much of what we do understand is the result of this sometimes elusive law in action.

Everything arises according to causes and conditions. This is the universal principle to which the Buddha awoke when sitting beneath the bodhi tree. It describes the origin of the myriad things, how they came to be, where they came from and how they function and move within the universe. Where there is a cause, there must be an effect. Specifically, particular kinds of causes in combination, produce specific effects. 'You reap what you sow' is a common expression to explain this relationship, as is the saying 'good things happen to good people' These are the simplest expressions of cause and effect.

The law of cause and effect is what orders the universe, determines the trajectory of our lives and the evolution of all phenomena. Much of what we do not understand is the result of some unknown cause and effect relationship. That is the other name for the law of cause and effect. Recognised as describing the natural rhythm of the universe and of our fates, the law of cause and effect is central to our practice – we must acknowledge, respect and revere it. Understanding the law provides a fuller grasp of the inner workings of the world, of ourselves and of our mind-nature.

There are two lessons we can derive from the fact that 'everything is contingent. The first is that the myriad things of the universe are all innately and essentially impermanent, and since there are also unlimited possibilities for how the unceasing dependent origination of phenomena might unfold, it is difficult to truly predict or control the trajectory of any phenomena. The second is that the origin and formation of the myriad things are both traceable, and they do not occur at random. How the myriad things appear in the present moment is decided by cause and effect.

Herein lies one of Dharma's most profound teachings. I contain you, you contain me, this contains that, that contains this – within impermanence there is permanence, within which there is impermanence. Buddhist masters often advise us to react to the phenomena we encounter throughout our daily lives with restraint, by reminding ourselves of the law of cause and effect, controlling our actions and words, and performing benevolent deeds in order to earn karmic merit. They also remind us that should this approach not go to plan, we must continue to view the situation through the lens of impermanence.

Life places each of us in countless situations and in front of countless different people on a daily basis, and each of those encounters itself is comprised of incalculable elements. Dependent origination is constant. New causes and conditions arise in every moment without our knowledge or notice. However, there are certain instances of cause and effect that we can track back through their unfolding, which suggests it is possible for us to control certain aspects of our lives by their dependent origination.

Here is an example of the law of cause and effect in action.

For a bountiful harvest, a farmer needs fertile soil, good quality seeds and favourable weather. They must also devote time and care to tending the crops and putting measures in place to protect them against pests. This is only a small slice of the gamut of tiny details they have to attend to if they are to have any hope of success. These elements combine to determine the dependent origination of a crop: whether or not, come autumn, the farmer can bring in a good harvest. There are so many factors at play in deciding how just a single phenomenon develops; and for it to go as we wish, we often need the majority to go in our favour.

By contrast, messing something up requires very little to go wrong for the whole thing to fall apart. For this reason, we must make a promise to ourselves not to expect things to always go our way or come together on their own. If we do not receive the karmic payoff we believe we deserve, we must not complain or lose our temper. For things to align in our favour has a much lower probability than otherwise. We must mentally prepare for all eventualities and face any outcome with equanimity while practicing gratitude and appreciation.

'He who touches pitch shall be defiled therewith.' Or as the Chinese say, 'Handling vermillion will mark you red; handling pitch will mark you black.' This is another description of cause and effect. Over thousands of years of civilisation, humanity has accumulated wide and varied experience. We have learned to recognise how certain actions lead to certain results. However, the tendency in ordinary society is to evaluate cause and effect based on notions of good and bad, benevolent and evil. This kind of dualist, differentiating thinking ignores the fact that no phenomena, or its causes or conditions, is absolute. As we have seen, there are too many and too diverse factors involved in every instance of origination for any absolute judgement to be applied. Therefore, as a methodology for relieving afflictions and suffering, an understanding of the law of cause and effect alone can only help us so far. In practice, it can only partially alleviate our suffering and afflictions, as without wisdom of emptiness, we are still likely to cling to expectations.

Origination is constantly happening around us. Every worldly phenomenon in every moment originates according to established causes and conditions, thereby producing an action of some sort, material or otherwise, which in turn causes a result. Our future depends on the origination occurring in the present moment. Our present has developed from origination in the past. Cause and effect runs through every aspect of our lives, from beginning to end, and determines our karma and fortune.

The scriptures teach us that causes are powerful determinants of manifestation, in fact they are its main driver; conditions are by comparison weaker and act as external, supplementary factors. When causes and conditions coalesce, origination occurs; when causes and conditions dissolve, a phenomenon comes to an end. It is a constant state of flux. What comes first is considered a cause, and what follows is considered a result, until it itself becomes a cause. Dependent origination implies emptiness, therefore at the core of cause and effect is emptiness. Causes and conditions are themselves dependent, conditional phenomena; they manifest in diverse ways and forms. This we can see for ourselves in our own lives and in the world around us. So, although cause and effect are empty, their manifestations are not illusory. The truth is, 'everything is illusory, apart from the manifestations of cause and effect.'

Every cause produces a corresponding effect; every effect has a corresponding cause. Good results derive from good causes and conditions; bad results derive from bad causes and conditions. 'As the boy is, so will be the man', they say. A person of life experience can often surmise based on a child's habits at three years old what that same child will be like at eighty. Of course, there is a lot of uncertainty about such a prediction, but this does not mean it is baseless. The above saying reflects how much importance we attach to the habits of children and also suggests just how difficult it is to change a habit once formed. The latter is particularly true of bad habits which strengthen our notion of self, leading to ever more suffering. There is no way of avoiding this chain of cause and effect.

Cause and effect is central to our daily lives. There is a reason why everything happens as it does. Through awareness, it is possible to identify the reason for a particular event. We start to notice how certain causes lead to certain results, or at least how certain causes make certain results more likely. If we can develop this kind of understanding for more aspects of our lives, then we will be better placed to decide what is the right response to life's events.

However, cause and effect relationships are often more challenging to identify than they seem, especially given how much of our days we spend with our heads in a fog. How do we expect to be able to perceive the reason behind things if we spend our lives in waking slumber? The task is made all the more difficult by our subjectivity. We each process and interpret the world in our own unique way, which means the reason I identify for something happening will differ from the one you settle on. While you focus on one set of causes, I might pick out another. There could also be countless unknown reasons neither of us has spotted, some which are chance factors and some of which may only have contributed to increasing the likelihood of the resulting phenomenon occurring. But there is no absolute cause, since behind every cause are more causes. Regardless, there is much value in observing cause and effect relationships. In doing so, we learn how to recognise then take action at the causal stage of a phenomenon, perhaps halting undesirable phenomena from manifesting.

Cause and effect explains the origin of all phenomena. Every area of life involves cause and effect relationships. In this chapter, I have chosen to look at diet and health to explore whether there is an inevitable cause and effect link between them. My hope is to show that cause and effect relationships are more complex than they seem.

In one story in Old Path White Clouds, Pasenadi asks the Buddha if he remembers when Pasenadi, after eating too much and becoming sleepy, went for a walk, only to bump into the Buddha standing on the same path. The Buddha laughs and replies, 'Yes, I remember, your Majesty. Majesty, simply eat less. Doing so will make your mind and body feel lighter, which will improve your ability to perform both your work of governing and your spiritual practice.' A Buddhist master once said that at least half the suffering in our life comes from a lack of mindfulness when we eat and drink. A bad diet is a hinderance to the Dharma practice and can bring harm to the body and mind. We must distinguish which foods and drinks are beneficial for our health, and which are harmful. We must learn how to eat and drink in a way that keeps the body and mind happy and healthy.

We should look at eating and drinking as part of our daily cultivation practice. Right mindfulness is key while doing either. It helps us to remove the self from the process and can leave the body feeling healthier and lighter. Cultivating body and mind together has complementary benefits. The opposite of mindful consumption is observable in the greediness rife in modern society. People are obsessed with eating large amounts of indulgent foods. It is a worrying trend that only feeds our notion of self and is bad for our physical health. China's economy has developed at an extraordinary speed in the past few decades, and people's quality of life has greatly improved. It used to be that only the rich could eat well, but it has now become common throughout the population to eat regular meals of meat, fish and seafood, accompanied by more fruits and drinks than the diners can reasonably consume. That nutrient rich meals are good for the health is an idea spread by businesspeople, when, to be frank, what they are selling is the idea that high protein, high fat and high calorie foods are good for you.

Modern society's pandemic of overeating is worrying. It feeds our notion of self and is bad for our physical health. ▶▶

Protein is a fundamental part of any diet. But precious protein can be found in abundance in rice, staples and vegetables. We need protein, but only in moderation. More is not necessarily better. In this age when access to protein is plentiful, excess consumption of protein only creates a burden for our bodies. Anyone who grows plants knows that water and fertiliser are necessary for their growth, but just as too little of either will stifle the plant, too much can have as bad an effect. It is important we remember that feeding ourselves can be much the same. Our bodies are only so large and our organs only so efficient. Eating more nutrient-dense, high protein foods only fills us with more nutrients than we can digest and absorb, and what we cannot absorb or dispel is retained in the body in some form or another, where it accumulates over time as fat, cholesterol and many other unwelcome waste nutrients. The result is bad health and, consequently, a bad cultivation practice.

We are not exempt from the law of cause and effect. The state of our health is directly connected with past and present originations. Air quality, cleanliness of water, access to food, movement, rest, seasonal changes, emotional state, genetics, alcohol consumption, a history of smoking, how much of the day we spend hunched over our computer or laid in bed looking at our phone, what time we go to sleep—these are some of the many factors that determine our health. We ordinary people lack the awareness to recognise the whole range of factors affecting our health, so this chapter aims to give a few suggestions for how we can better keep tabs on the causal relationship between consumption and health.

As far as I am concerned, two of the best markers for good health are restful sleep and normal bowel movements. Deep sleep indicates normal digestive function and blood production as well as balanced energy and calorie intake. Bad sleep often either signals unusual digestion and blood production or an excess energy and calorie intake, or both. 'An uncomfortable spleen or stomach makes for uneasy sleep,' Traditional Chinese Medicine (TCM) tells us; add to which an excess of energy and calories, and it is inevitable that our body will feel agitated, a state in which restful sleep becomes elusive. Bad sleep can quickly devolve into insomnia, so it is important that we monitor our habits.

Normal bowel movements indicate a healthy stomach and intestines and good digestion. If we eat a lot yet have very little, or even no, diarrhoea, food is being retained in our body, which is a cause for concern. Other symptoms of unhealthy bowels are bloody piles or blood in our stool. Both call for immediate attention. Our bloodstream nourishes our body, and prolonged loss of blood can cause us considerable harm. Anaemia or other hard-to-predict illnesses could follow if we do not take action. The health of our body relies on the function of our digestive system and on the quality of our sleep, which can also affect each other.

A healthy stomach and spleen not only flushes our bodies of unwanted build-up, more importantly, it helps to maintain our internal equilibrium. When our body and organs are in balance, we enjoy high quality sleep, and when we are sleeping well, we produce high quality blood. Blood is key to the proper function of the body, and clean blood is an important standard for health. For example, young farm workers in the countryside used to eat rice for every meal and had very little chance to consume junk food or fizzy drinks, so their blood remained clean and plentiful, and their cheeks were as rosy as two apples.

Blood production is an important part of the system for maintaining physical health, one we must not overlook. Good blood production is dependent on the normal function of our stomach and spleen, and on good sleep. The stomach and spleen are widely known to be key organs when it comes to achieving healthy digestion, nutrient absorption and blood production; rice and flour are also considered important sources of nutrients for promoting good blood production. So, we must eat more rice- and flour-based products and take good care of our stomach and spleen to guarantee good sleep. This, in turn, will keep our blood clean. Below, we continue to look at these markers of good health by exploring, using my own insights, the causal relationship between consumption and our stomach and spleen health, and between stomach and spleen health and general health.

TCM refers to the stomach and spleen as the 'root of postnatal life', because of the organs' essential role in our biochemistry. They process and extract the nutrients we need from food and convert them into blood. 'The centre of the body receives qi and extracts its juices, changing and transforming them to red: what we call blood.' Rice and flour are rich in starch and contain protein, vitamins, fat and other nutrients. Starch, once digested in the stomach, is converted into energy and blood by the stomach and spleen. So, for fresh blood production, we need the spleen and stomach to function effectively, which healthy sleep habits can promote.

Blood is, in many ways, the source of life. It flows through our body like a river, carrying nutrients to every part of it. Clean blood, you could say, nourishes our body, while unclean blood full of toxins negatively affects our health. It is rare for people to pay much attention to the quality of the blood their body is producing, and often by the time we realise there is a problem, it is too late. Diabetes, high blood pressure, psoriasis, lupus, gout, rheumatoid arthritis, leukaemia, cancer – any one of these illnesses could strike, whether we have problems with blood production, diet, the stomach and spleen, sleep or our bowel movements.

Learning about the problems caused by overconsumption early on can help us to approach our diet with due awareness. Years of indulgence in nutrient-dense, high protein diets of difficult-to-digest foods builds up non-digested materials in the body, which makes the blood thick and viscous. When the body no longer has a way of properly storing these excess materials, they will find their own route out. If persistent bad digestion and bowel movements are the problem, the materials will leave the system through the skin in the form of a skin disease. While a year and a half of allowing this build up to continue might only produce minor skin problems, ten or more years of wrong food choices can risks more serious diseases developing, like psoriasis, scleroderma or skin lupus.

Human biological systems are incredibly complex in their individual makeup and in how they interact with one another. Sometimes, unbeknownst to us, excess materials will begin to accumulate within the body rather than try to leave, often taking the form of a tumour or tumours of some sort. A tumour formed through a decade of bad diet habits can starts to rot, denature and stink, and eventually could become cancerous. Often, if allowed to develop into the later stages of growth, a cancerous tumour will rapidly spread, in a process called metastasis.

Excess materials can also accumulate throughout the body in various parts simultaneously—as opposed to in a single location—sometimes even building up in the blood. You can imagine, all of those undigested nutrients are bound to thicken the blood, slowing flow and likely worsening the function of the stomach and the spleen, which in turn will thicken the blood further. It is a vicious cycle. When the blood flows through certain parts of the body now, through the joints for example, it will slow or stop, leading to gout or rheumatoid arthritis.

Then there is diabetes, which is tied to high-protein consumption. It is known as a 'rich man's disease', since it used to only be rich people with indulgent lifestyles that contracted it. Diabetics have excess stores of protein distributed throughout their bodies, in the legs in particular. If you prick the feet or legs of a sufferer of end-stage diabetes, the skin will immediately break. It is like poking a boiled egg that has been peeled. One indicator of diabetic kidney damage is protein in the urine, or proteinuria. This is why the urine of diabetics attracts lots of ants. Clearly, if we do not bring a diet of excess into check, the consequences will be dire.

Key to the health of the body is 'looking after the spleen and stomach'. A damaged stomach or spleen can be the cause for any number of diseases. If they are functioning well, our other organs will also function well. So, with our health in mind, we must take control of what we put in our mouths, making sure that our diet equips our stomach and spleen to digest food and extract nutrients with the utmost efficiency and to clear out any unwanted excess materials lingering in the body. This will bring our energy and calorie levels into balance, improve our sleep and, with the help of good rest, promote higher quality blood production, keeping us strong and resistant to disease.

Everything we eat and drink – including soda pop, soup, junk food, fruit and red and white meats – all passes through our mouths and journey down our bodies into stomach. At a guess, we probably eat about enough food a day to fill a bucket. Greedy, overindulgent eating overburdens the stomach and spleen, causing them harm in the long run. Every disease or illness we develop is linked to our stomach and spleen and our diet, whether directly or indirectly.

The mouth is where this process begins, it is the channel through which we fuel our being. You can imagine how weak we would become if we did not put food into our mouths every day, how our bodies would slowly fail and deteriorate. Meeting our body's nutritional needs with our consumption gives us strength and energy, it prepares us to face the day, but giving in to our desires and eating excessively is another story. It leaves us heavy and ages us. Good dietary choices, then, ensure the proper function of the stomach, spleen and other organs as well as of the urinary system, reproductive system and excretory system. Persistent bad dietary choices damage stomach and spleen and lead to problems elsewhere in the body. Thousands of years of learning have allowed us to identify and innovate countless foods that suit our constitution and with which, financial situation permitting, we can stock our pantries and fill the dinner table. So, what is a reasonable diet? What form of consumption suits us? The answers to these questions cannot be given in full here, but suffice to say that looking after the stomach and spleen should be a daily concern in our cultivation.

How we look can after these essential organs is explained below. First, do not overindulge, either in terms of quantity or richness of food. Second, base your meals around rice, noodles, flour-based goods, vegetables and eggs, all foods a weakened stomach or spleen can easily handle. What are other easily digestible foods? Foods that at room temperature go bad relatively quickly, whether they have been cooked or not. Cooked rice, noodles, steamed buns and dumplings all spoil after only a short time at room temperature, a sign that they are good foods, not only for promoting blood production, but for being easily digestible.

Vegetables also spoil easily and suit being cooked. Our history and evolution shows that humans need cooked food, as it is easier to digest and absorb nutrients from than the alternative. Cooked vegetables, in particular, are very important to our diet. They provide plant proteins, vitamins, trace elements and fibre, and are low in calories. Eating vegetables leaves us feeling comfortable and aids our excretions. As does eating eggs, which play an important role in our diet since they contain vitamins, iron, calcium and high-quality protein. Combined with rice, noodles and vegetables, they complete our daily nutritional requirements, and if on occasion we pair them with a little fish or meat, then even better. Thousands of years of human survival prove that by centring our eating habits around these foods, we have no need to worry about nutrition.

It is a problem requiring attention that cold and raw foods have increased in popularity as a way of enriching the textural experience of a meal. But uncooked foods only burden the digestive system with extra work. For this reason, we should avoid them in particular when already ill, as is advised in many TCM manuals. In the summer months, when the weather is much warmer, a little fruit to refresh yourself is fine. But remember, the stomach and spleen like warm and hot foods. Even room temperature foods, which were warm but have been left to cool, can be problematic, as can cool water. We have all experienced how good it feels to wash our hands with hot water, even if we forget to use soap. By the same logic, drinking warm water rehydrates us better than cool water and helps to clean out our digestive system. Two birds with one stone.

We must also avoid high protein and difficult-to-digest meat, junk food and overly-processed drinks when our stomach and spleen are already in suboptimal states. Soda pop can destroy a person's health and has already wreaked havoc on the health of whole generations – this isn't as farfetched as it might sound. It is a common attitude to think we know what might damage our health, but have we really grasped just how harmful certain foods can be?

Buddhist Dharma explains that 'Bodhisattvas respect causes'. They understand which causes produce which effects and, therefore, maintain correct mindfulness and the right view at all times in order to monitor their actions. By comparison, we laypeople have disordered thoughts. We spend our lives sleepwalking, unaware of ourselves and our surroundings and of the causal relationships between things. We are not bodhisattvas. We see bad results unfold before us and only then do we know fear, by which point there is nothing we can do. So, we must learn to recognise the causal relationships to phenomena and cultivate a more profound insight into our lives and work.

Self-interest means that everyone has desires. The desire to eat and drink 'well' is hard to resist. Adults and children alike easily falter in their self-control when a plate of delicious food or a bag of their favourite junk food is placed before them. Food tempts and seduces us into unrestrained indulgence. We need to establish a strong awareness of that side of ourselves and, when we feel our self-restraint slipping, choose to remove ourselves from temptation. This is a habit we must teach our children. Mindfulness around food is the path to better physical, mental and spiritual health.

I have a child myself, so the health of our youngest generation is a concern that is close to my heart. Unfortunately, excessive consumption is a problem that greatly affects our youth, as well as the rest us, to a worrying degree. Nowadays, most guardians dedicate a lot of energy to thinking about and planning their children's diet, yet kindergartens continue to overfeed students. A typical schedule of meals at a kindergarten in China currently begins with breakfast at quarter past eight. After that, the children do not have to wait long before their next meal at ten a.m. during break-time (some fruit or a carton of milk), then lunch at half past eleven (meat and fish with soup), then a post nap top-up at three (rice porridge, noodles, bread or sweetcorn) and then, depending on the school, maybe an extra meal of unlimited fruit at four. Children, of course, like to eat and do so happily. In fact, this kind of schedule often has the approval of both children and guardians.

It is natural for children to enjoy eating; it is built into our survival instinct. If there is food in front of them, they will eat; if there is a drink nearby, they will drink. If not curbed, this habit can quickly turn a child into a serial snacker, who eats very little during proper mealtimes besides meat or other less essential food groups. The short time between meals or snacks does not give the food enough time to be fully digested before more food is consumed, so the digestive system tires out. As we know, it is a precarious time for the health of our body when the spleen and stomach are not in tip-top shape. It could mean contracting a cold or a fever, developing a skin disease or suffering organ failure or halted blood production.

The problem is not helped when, after taking in plenty of nutrition at kindergarten, the children file home at half past four and the next stage of the consumption relay begins. Some are barely out of the school gate when their guardians hand them more food which they might eat as they walk. Then at home the evening meal awaits them. By this point, the children hardly have an appetite and quickly abandon dinner, telling their guardian they are full or don't want to eat anymore, which annoys the parents, who might threaten the children to eat more or force them to eat something, while the child tries to get away.

A child is in the early stages of development. Their intestines are narrow and their stomach small. They do not have space inside them for so much food. Yet they are force-fed throughout the day all the same. If we paid attention, we would notice that we

107

adults are far from innocent in this process, and many of us overeat too. There is an obsessiveness to this kind of eating, compulsively keeping the digestive system in an active state. You can imagine how inefficient this leaves the organs and the damage it will inevitably cause them, which in turn means problems for the rest of the organs.

We should also know that regular overeating pushes our energy and calorie levels beyond what is recommended, which stops the body from being able to relax. For this reason, the quality of sleep that today's children are used to getting compared with previous generations of young people is worryingly low. There are large numbers of children who struggle to sleep well or who struggle to fall asleep before the early morning. For some, this condition becomes as severe as insomnia, and they barely sleep at all. Without adequate sleep, our blood production faculties plummet, and a chain of other problems follow. Colds, fevers, a runny nose, sneezing and skin diseases are among the more common issues that might result, but some unlucky children contract serious, unexpected illnesses. Whatever the case, our 'causal conditions' are to blame; it is a guardian's responsibility to not let their children suffer from sickness.

Another question that troubles guardians is whether or not to send a child to school when they have a slight cough or runny nose. They are not quite sick – a little careful living for a short while and they'll quickly get better – but sending them to school, where lunch could include chicken legs, fish soup, dumplings, fruit, cake, milk and much more, might worsen their condition. As I understand it, a child in less-than-perfect-health requires a modified diet. The simpler, the better. Eating too much food or too rich food puts strain on the body, as it has to dedicate energy to digestion while also trying to recover from the existing sickness. Such eating risks pushing the coughs and sneezes into fever territory.

Generally speaking, people coddle their children too much nowadays. Grandparents are particularly bad offenders in this regard, their expectations for what their darlings should eat often leaving even schools and nurseries wanting. Our children are being overfed from every direction. The most obvious indicators of this trend are obesity and excessive skinniness. The former results from nutrients being converted into fat, the latter from a badly functioning digestive system, which struggles to absorb the necessary nutrients from food, causing the blood to thicken.

If hidden risks and damage to our children's bodily health are something guardians should be looking out for, then harm to their mental health—their mind-nature—requires even greater vigilance. Overconsumption is a form of nourishing the self, it can only result in a selfish, self-centred disposition. This way of being might become the default for a child by the time they are an adult if the habit is not curbed early on. An adult whose young selfishness was not brought under control is prone to consider themself the priority over others in all situations, including their partner, parents and other family members, flipping the usual family hierarchy on its head. This kind of inverted family dynamic is fertile ground for suffering. As a child becomes more selfish and self-centred, their parents feel more and more as though they did the heavy lifting of a stone only to drop it on their own foot. Once ingrained, a habit or disposition is difficult to break, and the longer before it is tackled, the more stubborn it becomes.

Think for a moment about what it meant to be healthy a few decades, or even centuries, ago. A healthy person's diet was centred around staple foods. They consumed a tiny proportion of the protein people do now, yet they lived significantly more active lives than the average modern human. Simply put, we eat too much and use too little energy. Our intake far exceeds what our bodies actually need, so we end up with stores of energy and calories that our body does not know what to do with. Overeating is only harmful; it offers no benefits. It not only damages our digestive system and affects sleep, but it also contributes to the growth of the self-nature of mind. Children that overeat will grow up to be adults that overeat and who are likely highly selfish and self-centred. Nurturing the self while trying to self-cultivate is a matter of one step forward, two steps back.

Everything is the result of causes and conditions. Diabetes, high blood pressure, lupus, cancer, any illness we might contract throughout life – they are all the result of causes and conditions. As is the course of an illness. From contraction to deterioration or recovery, there are countless factors at play, some of which we might be aware of, and others may never have occurred to us. They all overlap and influence one another. This is why it isn't uncommon for specialists to give a general diagnosis of the nature of a problem, which can complicate finding a cure and efforts at prevention. Unfortunately, without a cure, the problem goes untreated, and the illness is likely to worsen. So, knowing a sickness' cause is very helpful when it comes to curing it and preventing its recurrence. Knowing the causes and conditions for a phenomenon is essential to us changing our behaviour and making the correct decisions in the future.

So, we have looked at how overeating is a key cause of illness in many people, and how, inversely, 'eating simple makes for easy digestion.' At the heart of simple eating is a desire to cleanse the body. Of course, for healthy young people or very active people, simple eating alone is perhaps not a good choice. Changing to simple eating is for regular overeaters, or people who want to go on a cleanse to bring their body back into balance.

Even after years of wanton overeating, we should not underestimate the power of simply kickstarting our awareness practice as the first step to changing our habits. Awareness of the damage we have been doing to our health, both physical and mental, is a simple trick to shift our perspective and begin making small dietary changes to bring our health under control by eating more staple foods: rice, flour-based goods, vegetables and eggs.

Simple eating can cleanse the body. If we can stick to our new diet a day a time, eating the recommended daily intake, our body will quickly start to restore its balance and our blood will thin, and very soon there will be noticeable results.

It is important that we realise that every instance of cause and effect is itself the result of an earlier cause. We alone are not to blame for our bad diet decisions. The greatest offenders are the diet cultures and beliefs about eating and certain foods that we are bombarded with from birth. Overeating, for example, is a problem that has grown out of three decades of abundance, which have seen people eat more and more and move less and less. My analysis is also, of course, somewhat reductive, since different regions, different people and different living conditions produce different ideas about diet. Moreover, everybody is different. We all have different bodies, so no single diet will meet the needs of all.

Above is an exploration of cause and effect within diet and health. Within Buddhism, for the law of cause and effect, what is most important is that, 'Good is rewarded with good, and bad with bad.' We may have noticed that benevolent behaviour stands out, while a benevolent mindset is subtle. Dharma greatly emphasizes the importance of mindset. It teaches that everything is a manifestation of the mind, that manifestations of the mind are more important than actual behaviour. So, wholly selfless acts bring great karmic reward, but benevolent acts driven by selfish intent are less meritorious. Of course, for the majority of us laypeople, it is normal to harbour selfish intent while helping others, or to have a differentiating mind. What we must be really wary of, then, is letting the self take control of our actions, regardless of how benevolent we believe them to be. This is why an understanding of the Dharmic law of cause and effect can only guide us toward partially solving our suffering and afflictions. True liberation requires that we embody non-self.

At this point in the book, readers might have a question: should we create good causes and conditions or avoid creating bad ones? Is it better that we follow the wisdom of emptiness and embrace causes and conditions as they are in the moment? This is without a doubt the hardest part of Buddhist Dharma to understand.

It is common for us to be willing to accept the causes and conditions that have our approval, and not those that don't. The latter often draw an emotional response that drives us to reject or try to avoid them. So, it is far from an easy thing for a person to calmly and happily follow the causes and conditions of the present moment at every moment. Only those of us in sync with non-self and free of differentiating tendencies can achieve this state of being. Such a person has realigned themselves with their essential nature, and their nature of mind has primacy over everything.

But we should still be conscious during our cultivation practice of creating good causal conditions and avoiding creating bad ones. This is a necessary part of every practitioner's self-cultivation. 'Good is rewarded with good, and bad with bad' – remember this law is eternally true.

CHAPTER EIGHT

Emptiness and Non-Self

When the Bodhisattva Guanyin finally gained a deep understanding of the supreme wisdom that is Prajna Paramita[4], the bodhisattva shone their light of awareness upon all things, internal and external, and realised that the five aggregates[5] – the skandhas of form, sensations, perceptions, mental activity and consciousness – were but illusory and empty at their core; at the same time, the bodhisattva awoke to the truth that the myriad things have emptiness and non-self as their essential nature, at which moment the bodhisattva attained nirvana and was liberated from all suffering.

Everything is the result of the coalescence and dissolution of causes and conditions. Such is the underlying principle of the universe and the key to understanding the true form of the myriad things – emptiness. As the essential nature of the myriad things, emptiness refers to the absence of any essential, inherent, independent aspect of selfhood. At its core is non-self. Where there is belief in selfhood, emptiness is difficult to understand. Only those beings that have attained a state of non-self can be considered to have aligned their being with emptiness.

112

Old Path White Clouds relates a story of when Rāhula, the eighteen-year-old son of Siddhārtha Gautama, the Buddha, received instruction from his father to look to the earth below his feet, to water and to fire and to emptiness to learn about the essence of non-self. The Buddha said, 'Rahula, learn from the earth. Whether people spread pure and fragrant flowers, perfume, or fresh milk on it, or discard filthy and foul-smelling faeces, urine, blood, mucus, or spit on it, the earth receives it all equally without clinging or aversion. When pleasant or unpleasant thoughts arise, don't let them entangle or enslave you.

'Learn from the water, Rahula,' he continued. 'When people wash dirty things in it, the water is not sad or disdainful. Learn from fire. Fire burns all things without discrimination. It is not ashamed to burn impure substances. Learn from the air. The air carries all fragrances, whether sweet or foul.'

What can we learn from the myriad things about emptiness and non-self? We should look to the myriad things of the universe, to the earth below our feet, to the water, to fire and the air, for examples of non-differentiating being; of being without expectations or attachments. Each of them abides by the causes and conditions of the present moment; they are non-self manifest. Therefore, they do not suffer. Humans, on the other hand, are peculiar entities. We are gifted with an advanced level of consciousness, with the ability to deliberate and create, gifts we have put the flourishing of ourselves and the world. However, as a result, we are prone to falling under the influence of the self.

4
    Referred to in Sanskrit as prajñā, this is insight into the true nature of reality. Prajñā pāramitā is the last of the Six Perfections

5
    Five Aggregates; that is, physical and mental phenomena experienced by humans that completely compose and explain the foundation of sentient beings' entire existence. The Five Aggregates include form (rūpa), sensations (vedanā), perceptions (samjñā), karmically formed impulses (also referred to as mental activity — saṃskāra), and consciousness (vijñāna.) They serve as the foundation of the Buddhist self-cultivation system, and adherents of Buddhism cannot under any circumstances stray from this principle in the course of their practice.

The more we allow the self to dictate our lives, the wealthier we are likely to become, however, our suffering is unlikely to lessen as a result. If we wish to lighten or remove entirely the suffering we experience in our lives, we have to learn from the essential nature of non-self within the myriad things and apply what we learn to embodying non-self; in other words, we should regularly try to adopt a mindset free of differentiating thought and attachments. This is the key to accepting origination and living in the present moment. So why is it important that we embody non-self? Understanding the existence of non-self is insufficient to liberate us from suffering. We must fully manifest our intrinsic nature of non-self if we wish to have any hope of ridding ourselves of suffering entirely, both in our behaviour and in our thinking. This is the natural path to happiness and peace.

There is a pop song by Jonathan Lee, Victor Wong and Wakin Chau that speaks to the living situation of the modern youth. The lyrics go: 'Things have been hard recently, things they've been tough. I can see no end in sight, not an end to this road, and looking back all I see is talent hot on my tail; Things have been hard recently, things they've been tough, in a strange city, where can I find hope, I already said goodbye to my hometown friends, and now I feel alone. Things have been hard recently, things they've been tough, working every day from seven til' nine, I have only half a head of hair left.'

For a lot of young people, this is how life is turning out. At best, their days leave them frustrated and tired; at worst, they suffer through every hour, from morning till night. Suffering is not unique to any generation, but each generation experiences its own unique set of troubles and challenges. Yet, still we feel the same as a result – we suffer. This is why, throughout the ages philosophers and psychologists have never stopped plumbing the depths of the question, 'How do we stop suffering?' The consensus is that suffering derives from desire, from allowing oneself to be controlled by things and bound by emotion. The more dependent we become on things and emotions, the more tightly they bind us. Philosophers and psychologists can all see that it is desire that causes humanity suffering and affliction. Each school of thought has prescribed its own method for escaping suffering, but most of these methods do not address the core of the issue.

On a relative level, the Dharmic theory of emptiness takes the universal principle as its basis. It deals with the essential nature of the myriad things and so gets right to the heart of suffering; it thus represents the highest realm of wisdom. Two millennia of practice show that the Dharmic theory of emptiness is a potent activator of our inner wisdom, helping us see right to the heart of things and to perceive their essential nature as well as our own mind's essential nature, which in turn will lessen and can even eradicate our suffering. Buddhist emptiness is therefore an effective medicine for curing humankind of its suffering. This reminds me of the film, The Legend of the Demon Cat, in which there is a line toward the end that has stuck with me, 'Dan Long, have you discovered how to not suffer any longer?' The director seems to be implying that the way to stop suffering is Buddhist Dharma.

But what is suffering? The answer is not so straightforward as you might think, since there are clear distinctions between the Buddhist view of suffering and that of secular society. The latter sees suffering as intense emotional discomfort, which derives from physical pain, psychological discontent or distress. Secular society focusses on the feeling of suffering but fails to identify its intrinsic cause. By comparison, Buddhism defines suffering as attachments to external phenomena. In other words, when something external takes hold of us in a way that leads to reliance and expectations, meaning we have lost our freedom of mind, we leave ourselves vulnerable to suffering when the causes and conditions around that thing change. Inversely, if we are free of attachments, expectations and dependencies, external phenomena cannot determine of emotional state and our mind can be free. Buddhism regards this as peace and happiness.

It is quite clear that the secular perspective on suffering focusses on surface feelings, while the Buddhist perspective looks deeper. Without a doubt, Buddhism has identified the crux of the problem of suffering. It teaches us that the root of suffering is attachment, at the core of which is the self. So, in order to cure ourselves of attachments and suffering, we must cure ourselves of the influence of the self. If we can do this, all attachments will disappear, and so will all suffering.

However, achieving this is easier said than done. As an independent entity, we may believe ourselves to possess an independent, intrinsic self. This is only natural. We all possess a self, and a unique self at that – this is the prevailing belief of mundane society. 'I' and 'self' are very simple concepts with a very simple function. For a lot of people, those of us who begin every sentence we speak in a day with 'I', they are a means of emphasising our uniqueness in relation to others. We believe that people speak with us because we possess a self, a perspective that only dooms us to suffer forevermore! Heavens, it is hard to understand how harmful such a simple thing can be. But the Buddha taught that it is true. At the core of all deluded views in the secular world is a belief in the existence of self.

We must remember that suffering is not the natural state of the universe, it is caused by an erroneous understanding of life. At its core is a belief in the existence of self, which leads to dualist, differentiating thinking and produces expectations and attachments. The notion of selfhood violates the essential nature of the myriad things. In fact, a person who has never clearly seen or experienced that their essential nature is non-self will forever remain self-centred, and suffering will follow them like a shadow.

As already mentioned in chapter four, when material phenomena in the universe move from a state of disorderliness to one of orderliness, they are acquiring energy, and when they undergo the reverse – entropy – they are expending energy. Our growth from birth into adulthood follows a tendency toward orderliness, as we gain energy from and learn skills to navigate our environment. Since the onus is on intake throughout this process, it is common that self-centredness characterises this period of life. The later years of life represent a process of expenditure – a tendency toward disorder – as we constantly dedicate our energy to our children, household and society. As I understand it, embracing this shift from a state of self-centredness to non-self is at this time of life the best option.

Throughout history, there are many examples of wise masters who spent their earlier years nurturing the self, before an experience of suffering and certain events showed them that it was best in middle-age or their later years to turn their focus toward non-self. Perhaps this shift is an inevitable part of life. It certainly represents the most significant turnaround we can experience. You can imagine that it is a fortunate thing to be able to embrace 'non-self' after decades of living convinced of their selfhood. But it is a tragedy when someone allows that belief in 'selfhood' to spiral into self-centredness.

Gifted with the cognition and intelligence we have, and with the potential for wisdom, we are prone to overestimating our importance and our position in the universe. It is essential that we realise that the universe is an interconnected system, of which we are a single part. Our place within it, just like the place of each of the myriad things, is determined by causes and conditions; that is to say, our rightful place is out of our hands. Yet, our deluded selves seem always to expect that the world should fit one hundred percent to our expectations. If this is the case, how do we ever expect to be satisfied? This is not the path to freedom.

Nothing in the universe is permanent. Everything external to us, whether ephemeral or abiding, is essentially empty. Like the reflection of a flower in a mirror, or the reflection of the moon in a river, it is illusory and impermanent. Regular concern for what is bound to vanish can only lead to loss and emotional turmoil. Acceptance of the essential nature of the myriad things allows us to keep our mind on non-self and can free us of our fetters to external things. This is how we achieve peace and quiet for our inner mind.

If we can fully recognize the emptiness, non-self and impermanence within the myriad things, we can regulate our state of mind and avoid overestimating ourselves or believing ourselves to be right at all times. We can put down our preconceived notions and stances, let go of our expectations and our attachments, and relinquish our notion of selfhood. We can live in alignment with and acceptance of the present causes and conditions and embody non-self in the present moment. Doing things without goals, expectations or selfish intent, with complete concentration on the task at hand is one manifestation of a state of non-self. Possessing a notion of selfhood brings with it attachments and expectations as well as a belief that we can control things. It represents resistance to the origination of the present moment, to the collective. By contrast, embodying non-self aligns us with collective existence, in which moment our mind becomes free and our awareness receptive to whatever messages our environment is relaying. In such moments, we may find ourselves in harmony with everything around us. This is true non-self.

The suffering and events we experience through our life from youth to middle age and beyond serve to awaken us to the need to shift our perspective from one based in 'selfhood' to one based in non-self. To do so represents the most significant turnaround in our lives. ▶▶

Non-self is the core of all the myriad things; it is the nature of all the myriad things. Emptiness is the universal principle; it is the true form and characteristic of the universe. As members of humankind, we must thank our nature of non-self for the knowledge it gives us to be able to search for the essence of things, respect the source of all being and serve our origin, thereby aligning ourselves with the universe and with collective existence.

The individual must respect and serve the collective. This is the natural order of things. It is the only way that an individual can embody non-self. An individual who is driven by the self can never achieve true respect and service for the collective.

The universe is the largest manifestation of collective existence. It evolved to what it is now, iteration by iteration, form by form, in line with causes and conditions, from an originary matter, which existed before the Big Bang, and it continues to do so. There was a point in that timeline, when the causes and conditions of the moment brought about the creation of Earth, which in the beginning was little more than stone, mud and magma. Only later did the lush and diverse world we know today come to be. The material that formed the universe aeons ago is the same material that became Earth and the same material that makes up everything on the planet.

So, everything on today's Earth – trees, birds, fish, humans – comprises its share of the original material. The source and exact nature of this material remains elusive, however we know for certain that it is real. The Buddha said that when the myriad things deform or disintegrate, they reunite with the original material. Like a drop of water in the ocean which becomes humidity in the air, then rises into the sky and binds with a speck of dust, which joins with other particulates and forms a cloud, which then becomes rain, which falls from the sky and eventually finds its way back to the ocean. If not during the first cycle, then at some point in its existence.

Regardless how many births and deaths, originations and ends a myriad thing has undergone, it will always return to its original source. It does so by way of each originary layer between the most recent iteration of the material and the very first one. Just like families have generations that extend back as far as humanity itself, from each of which the next generation is born, the myriad things have evolved from previous manifestations of matter, each one closer to the original source the further back you look. Every family also forms part of a bigger lineage; that of a village, for example, or a city or a country, and it the individual's responsibility to fulfil our role within each. We should respect and serve the collective, at every level. This is the fundamental basis of human community.

The reason for this is that, like the myriad things, our existence is mutually dependent on that of others within the collective. The myriad things, ourselves included, are part of a single whole, derived from the same originary material, of which we are all simply a tiny part. Essentially, we belong to a collective, which everything we have or identify with also comes from. Everything we possess will sooner or later return to this collective. Once our lives have run their course, we too return to merge with it. So, non-self is an essential characteristic of the myriad phenomena; non-self is the right path; it is the great way; it is the universal principle.

At the relative level, it is best that we think of the human self-nature of mind as innate, a quality we nurture, unintentionally or otherwise, through our interactions with our environment after birth. Often, this sees the self grow plump, making us ever more selfish and self-centred. There is a point at which this selfishness becomes so deeply ingrained in our being that to rid ourselves of it can seem all but impossible. The journey to successfully changing our ways begins, I believe, with an important insight: experience of the nature of the self, its true form, and how it relates to the collective. Correct cognition of the self is necessary for an individual to understand how they fit into the collective. Once we have that, we can vow to relinquish the self and strive to live according to the value of non-self.

When we successfully situate ourselves in the natural order of things as an individual cog within the collective we might experience a fleeting sense of insignificance, perhaps even of 'ego-death'. 'Ego-death' is a state that closely resembles what it feels like to embody non-self. Insight into our own insignificance can bring up feelings of fear as well as reverence and awe. It is the clearest window we can have as an individual into the natural might and sacredness of the collective. In many ways, this is a self-perpetuating cycle of realisation. Once we acknowledge the collective's status relative to ourselves, our respect for, acceptance of and willingness to serve the collective will grow, and our sense of individuality and self-centredness will shrink, until we have fully manifested the essential nature of non-self. Having a better understanding of the collective is a big step toward shifting one's mental default to that of collective thought, which is a mode of thinking readily suited to accepting origination and living in the moment.

The better we understand the natural order of the collective universe, the more deeply we will experience every phenomenon as having its good and its bad aspects, which complement and depend on each other, and evolve and exchange in accordance with origination. Each of the myriad things has its place and manifests as origination dictates in the moment. As we start to clearly see the true nature of the world around us, that good and bad are part of it and that they are beyond our control, as is the origination and cessation of every phenomenon, we will gradually find it easier to let go of expectations and attachments.

We live in the grace of the universal collective. Think about it. Through a harmony of causes and conditions, the universe gave us life. It gave us the wherewithal and ability to live self-sufficiently. It put a wise head on our shoulders. It permitted us decades of life to do with as we wish. When we reach old age and our bodies and minds are failing us, it will return us to our original state and we can begin again. All of this is thanks to the harmony of origination. The natural universe is the root source of humankind's means to survive. Humans are only one material form within the everchanging state of the universe. We are only passers-through in the full timeline of existence.

The universe is the largest manifestation of the collective. Each person is only a tiny part of that collective. We should therefore maintain a humble mindset. When things go our way, we must not become arrogant and profligate. When things do not go our way, we must not lose heart. Accept origination, selflessly; embrace the natural changes of the universe in every moment; and align ourselves with nature. Be like a drop of water in the ocean; change with the tides. This is the natural order of things. Dependent origination explains why everything is emptiness, everything is non-self. It is a central concept of Buddhist Dharma. The *Heart Sutra* provides instruction on emptiness and non-self. When the Bodhisattva Guanyin finally gained a deep understanding of the supreme wisdom that is Prajna Paramita, the bodhisattva shone their light of awareness upon all things, internal and external, and realised that the five aggregates – the skandhas of form, sensations, perceptions, mental activity and consciousness – were but illusory and empty at their core; at the same time, the bodhisattva awoke to the truth that the myriad things have emptiness and non-self as their essential natures, at which moment the bodhisattva attained nirvana and was liberated from all suffering. When a person sees clearly to the essential nature of the myriad things, and aligns themselves with the natural state of the universe, with emptiness and non-self, they begin to see emptiness and non-self in everything.

'Form is no different from emptiness; emptiness is no different from form. Form is emptiness; emptiness is form.' Our six sense organs – the eyes, ears, nose, tongue, body, and mind – receive countless pieces of information of six kinds – visual form, sound, smell, taste, touch and phenomenal. This information sparks a sensation within us, which give rise to perceptions, which lead to mental activity, which accumulates as consciousness. When we have embraced the emptiness and non-self of all things, we realise that each of these building blocks of the human experience is itself empty and essentially non-self. Our entire existence appears integrated with that of the universe, and it is free of suffering. No longer must we cycle through suffering, arising, cessation and practice; aging, sickness and death no longer pose us any problem.

When we deeply understand Prajna Paramita and perceive clearly the essential nature of the myriad things, aligning ourselves with it and maintaining a state of emptiness and non-self, through observing our external and internal world in order to keep deluded and misleading thoughts and expectations away, we live without fear. This is the wisdom at the heart of the theory of emptiness and non-self, a wisdom that is ours to harness by cultivating the Dharmic method. The *Heart Sutra* represents the core teachings of the *Mahāyāna Mahāparinirvāṇa Sūtra* and emptiness and non-self are at its core.

'Form is no different from emptiness; emptiness is no different from form. Form is emptiness; emptiness is form.' There are various and sundry interpretations of this sentence from the Heart Sutra. My understanding is that 'form' and 'emptiness' are the operative words in the teaching. 'Form' refers to the myriad external phenomena of the universe; 'emptiness' refers to their essential nature of non-self. The myriad phenomena of the universe are the result of the alignment and dissolution of causes and conditions; it is from this origin that they derive their essential nature of emptiness. Everything is emptiness. Everything lacks inherent, independent selfhood. However, the essential nature of the myriad things does not equate exactly with simply pointing out the absence of any inherent, independent existence. What's more, the external appearance of a thing is as much a part of it as its essential nature. Hence the saying, 'Form is no different from emptiness; emptiness is no different from form.' The essential nature of the myriad things is that they are absent any inherent, independent existence, while the absence of such an existence only explains the essential nature of the myriad in readily understandable terms. The statement that 'form is emptiness, emptiness is form' serves to emphasise the relationship between 'form' and 'emptiness'.

Since each one of the five aggregates is also the result of the alignment of causes and conditions, some of which are represented by its preceding aggregate, it too has no inherent essential aspect. Everything is emptiness, everything lacks independent existence. 'O Śāriputra, the material form is no different from emptiness, the material form is the same as emptiness, and emptiness the same as the material form. The other aggregates – sensations, perceptions, mental activity, consciousness – are the same way.' This short passage succinctly and precisely expresses the relationship between the essential nature of the aggregates, 'the emptiness of all phenomena', and the universal absence of any inherent, independent existence. It is a sentence we should keep close to our hearts.

The Buddha also provided important instructions about emptiness and non-self in the *Diamond Sutra*, in which he again gives a high evaluation of their importance. The Buddha said that 'when bodhisattvas practice charity, they should not abide [in the notion that they are practicing charity]. This is what is called 'practicing charity while not abiding in form,' and 'practicing charity while not abiding in sound, odour, taste, touch, or conceptions.' Why? If bodhisattvas practice charity while not abiding in signs of charity, their merit will be incalculable. Also, 'they should give rise to the pure aspiration in this way: they should not give rise to the aspiration while abiding in form. They should not give rise to the aspiration while abiding in sound, odour, taste, touch, or concepts. They should give rise to the aspiration while not abiding in anything' and, 'bodhisattvas should free themselves from all notions and arouse the aspiration for peerless perfect enlightenment. They should not arouse this aspiration while abiding in form, and they should not arouse this aspiration while abiding in sound, odour, taste, touch, or conceptualization. They should give rise to the aspiration that has no abode. If the mind abides, then this is not abiding. Therefore I say that the mind of the bodhisattvas should not abide in the form of charity.'

Consider for a moment the 84,000 methods laid out by the

Buddha in order to assist sentient beings on their journeys toward Buddhahood. Each one is designed to help us to cleanse ourselves of any habits which are driven by the self-nature of mind, thereby assisting us to enter into the realm of emptiness and non-self. Non-self is the fundamental practice. Only those who have embodied non-self can set foot on the other shore and achieve liberation.

Non-self represents the core concept of Chan Buddhism, and is also essential to the Chan state. Specifically, 'Realising one's nature of mind in order to attain Buddhahood through enlightenment' is the main objective of Chinese Chan Buddhism, which I understand as realising one's mind has two meanings. One is to understand the true mind, and the other is to let light and space into one's mind. The process of 'realising one's mind' is one of removing the dirt of bad habits and purifying the mind of the influence of the self. Once our mind becomes clear to us, of course its true nature will become manifest. 'Realising one's nature' also has two meanings: one is to perceive the internal nature of non-self within us, and the other is to manifest that nature of non-self.

The Chan approach to practicing and realising non-self is the most direct. The school's cultivation practices all point practitioners toward the present moment and non-self with constant reminders of their importance. The Chan notion of non-self is neither the past non-self nor future non-self, it is the non-self of the present moment. This is a highly important distinction, and is central to Chan Buddhism. Align oneself with the present moment and reflect the present moment at all times. The Chan state is therefore the embodiment of non-self in the present.

Chan is one of the schools of Chinese Buddhism. Master Bodhidharma introduced Chan Buddhism to China. He wrote a number of Buddhist treatises which played an important role in its transmission. At their core they revolve around how to realize one's mind and nature. Realizing one's mind is necessary before one can realize one's nature. Once the mind is clear, it becomes

126

easy to perceive our nature. Below I have handpicked certain of Bodhidharma's teachings about realizing one's nature, from his works, *Treatise on the Transmission, Treatise on Realizing the Nature, Treatise on Refuting Appearances,* and *Treatise on the Two Entrances* and *Four Practices.* I recommend that readers slow down through this section in order to experience the full breadth of the Master's meaning. Perhaps after reading these passages, you will have a greater understanding of the non-self nature of mind.

• 'The mind is the root from which all things grow; everything grows from the mind.'

• 'If you understand the mind then cultivating the way will come easy.'

• 'Without an understanding of the mind, no amount of hard work will reap results.'

• 'Bodhisattvas and mahasattvas who understand deeply Prajna Paramita are able to see the essential emptiness and non-self in the four elements and five aggregates.'

• 'Karma produced from a defiled mind binds a person to ordinariness, sinking them into the three realms and leading to suffering in many unthinkable ways.'

• 'Free from defilement, one is a sage who avoids suffering and has nirvana within their reach.'

• 'All karmic suffering is brought about by the mind, but if one can take control of their mind, they will be able to keep away from evil and corrupting influences.'

• 'If one wishes to reach the Buddha land, one must purify one's mind.'

• 'Once the mind is purified, the Pure land of the Buddha awaits.'

- 'The wise allow things to change without changing themselves, thereby making no assessment of good or bad; the ignorant strive to change themselves without considering external conditions, thereby becoming tied to considerations about whether or not the situation is favourable.'

- 'If someone hopes to achieve Buddhahood, they must realize their nature. To realize one's nature is to discover the Buddha within; otherwise, one will remain an ordinary, sentient being.'

- 'Both the Buddha and Maitreya spoke only of realising the nature of things; the many scriptures and treatises speak only of understanding the mind.'

- 'A person who has not realised their nature can understand all of the scriptures and treatises, but they will never be anything but an ordinary person; what they have learnt is not Dharma.'

- 'The person who has realised their nature can unlock the wisdom within the twelve central scriptures.'

- 'Buddha nature is the mind; the mind is Buddha nature. The Buddha is the way, the way is Chan. To realise one's nature is to achieve Chan; if one cannot realise one's nature, then Chan is unattainable.'

- 'For the person who has truly realised their nature, everything becomes clear, and there is no more for them to realise. They already see each of the ten directions, the whole world, for what it is, yet it is just like they have seen nothing at all. The ordinary person has deluded thoughts on seeing anything; true seeing is to have all perception quieten and find oneself with nothing to perceive.'

- 'Thinking as a sentient being results in the loss of Dharmic insight; quieting the mind as a sentient being is the key to awakening Dharmic insight, since Dharmic wisdom is obfuscated by the workings of the mind. If one can stop the mind from having thoughts, then the mind will enter into the realm of emptiness and every thought will dissolve into quiet. Every moment thereafter is spent in the kingdom of the Buddha. If the mind is endlessly thinking, it can never achieve quiet, and every thought produces action and restlessness, turning every moment into hell.'

- 'The mind that achieves nirvana does not realise it exists in nirvana. If one believes they have perceived nirvana, they are wrong.'

If we have nothing on our mind, our mind will linger on nothing. A single flower opens into five petals, ultimately completing itself. The wisdom of Chan comes from the universal principle, from the natural order of things. It comes from the essence of emptiness, from the non-self within all the myriad things. Where there is self, there are attachments, and with attachments come deluded ideas, which lead to suffering. Non-self means no-thought; no-thought is the right state of mind to have. The Sixth Platform Sutra says, 'To keep our mind free from defilement under all circumstances is called 'no-thought'. The Sixth Patriarch Hui Neng upheld no-thought as his most important teaching. He taught his disciples, 'Our mind should stand aloof from circumstances, and on no account should we allow circumstances to influence the function of our mind.' Freedom and quiescence await, free from attachments and the shackles of external influences.

Both the Buddha and Maitreya spoke only of realising the nature of things; the person who has realised their nature can unlock the wisdom within the twelve central scriptures. ◄◄

Master Bodhidharma attached great importance to 'realising one's nature'. In his treatises, he dedicates a lot of space to providing instruction on how to achieve just that. This is how I understand the concept: the core of Buddhist cultivation is realising one's nature, which can be achieved at two levels. One is realising the essential nature of other phenomena, and the other is to realise the essential nature of the mind. The essential nature of all phenomena and of the mind is non-self, which is our Buddha nature, the latent potential within each of us to become a Buddha. Although the focus of these two possibilities is different, they are fundamentally the same. Chan Buddhism avoids any complex teachings and aims to show practitioners the most direct route to awakening. This is why Bodhidharma's writings focus on realising the 'essential nature of the mind'. If you have realised the essential nature of the mind, you have all but grasped the essential nature of all phenomena. Realising the essential nature of the mind is by far the most important of the two since everything is a manifestation of the mind. The quality of the mind is the quality of one's life. The state of your mind determines the state of your life.

Bodhidharma said that if we cannot perceive our nature, then to shave our heads and don robes does not make us Buddhist; if we cannot perceive our nature, then we cannot guide others in the ways of Buddhism; if we cannot perceive our nature, then neither chanting the names of the Buddha, reading scripture, following a vegetarian diet nor upholding precepts will benefit our cultivation; if we cannot perceive our nature, then regardless of our knowledge of the scriptures it is useless; if we cannot perceive our nature, we will be lost until the end of our days, searching desperately for the Buddha in the external world, to no avail; if we cannot perceive our nature, then we have no chance of walking the path of Buddhahood. Seeing to our essential nature is to have achieved Chan; if we cannot perceive our nature, Chan is out of our reach. Should we be well learned in the scriptures and teachings of Buddhism, if we cannot perceive our nature, we will remain an ordinary sentient being, and the teachings we have learnt are not the Dharma. If we perceive our nature, we can attain Buddhahood; if we cannot, we remain an ordinary, sentient being. Outside our nature there is no Buddha, the Buddha is our nature; our nature is our mind, which is the Buddha, which is the Way, which is Chan. Seeing to our essential nature, this is Chan.

How can we realise our nature? Master Bodhidharma taught that the mind is the Buddha, and the Buddha is our nature. Realising our nature is a matter of perceiving the essential nature of our mind, which is Buddha nature, an innate aspect of humankind, a permanent, immutable nature. After years of accumulating practice and wisdom, a cultivator may suddenly awaken to the intrinsic nature of non-self within, to the Buddha nature dormant within them, at which point the attendant qualities of the practitioner will come to the fore. As I understand it, this is what the Buddha calls 'enlightenment', or 'realising one's nature'. For those of us who consciously search for the nature of our mind, it does not matter what occupation we have, how much time we might spend or what environment we live in. The key to realising our nature is understanding our mind and perceiving the true essence of the world around us and the world within us. We must maintain a state of awareness at all times, and sooner or later, the essential nature of the mind will become clear and manifest.

Realising our nature is not necessarily something we must shut ourselves away in isolation or undergo daily Chan study in order to achieve. We can also achieve enlightenment in our daily lives, after an epiphany following a disagreement, for example, or entirely by surprise following some unremarkable event. In short, as long as we practice awareness, and strive to notice the essential nature of all things and our mind in our day to day, the day will eventually come when we realise and manifest the nature of our mind.

Of course, realising our nature does not solve everything. It is not the end of the journey quite yet. Just as many of us in our current practice have aligned our perspectives with the right view of non-self but have not achieved a mind of 'non-self' or aligned our behaviour with 'non-self', and therefore have not embodied non-self, so, after realising our nature, we must start to practice embodying 'the non-self nature of mind' and 'Buddha nature'. The more fully we can achieve this, the further behind us we can put our suffering and nearer we get to the other shore.

The Buddha said that if a person can attain enlightenment and freedom from suffering, they will see both the good and beautiful side of things and the bad and ugly side of things as empty and impermanent. They will see that within each there is contained all good and bad, all beautiful and ugly, and they will no longer be obsessed with pursuing the good and the beautiful, nor will they reject or resist the bad and ugly. A liberated person sees to the essential nature of all things. They transcend good and bad, ugly and beautiful; they know that everything is a product of the mind.

In the Buddha's mind, everyone possesses the potential for enlightenment and for achieving liberation from suffering, because everyone contains Buddha nature within their mind. Dharma teaches that the reason sentient beings often have not manifested our nature of non-self is that the self has obfuscated it. This is a matter of a deluded mind and deluded views covering the true nature of our mind. If we can maintain the right view of 'non-self' and remain aware, then the light of our awareness will gradually shine on and cleanse us of the self, allowing our non-self and Buddha nature to manifest.

Buddha is mind; the mind is the Buddha; Buddha nature is the essential nature of the mind; the essential nature of the mind is Buddha nature. How can we better align our nature of mind with the Buddha nature of mind? The *Diamond Sutra* contains an important lesson. 'The bodhisattvas and mahasattvas should give rise to the pure aspiration in this way: they should not give rise to the aspiration while abiding in form. They should not give rise to the aspiration while abiding in sound, odour, taste, touch, or concepts. They should give rise to the aspiration while not abiding in anything.' 'The bodhisattvas should free themselves from all notions and arouse the aspiration for peerless perfect enlightenment. They should not arouse this aspiration while abiding in form, and they should not arouse this aspiration while abiding in sound, odour, taste, touch, or conceptualization. They should give rise to the aspiration that has no abode. If the mind abides, then this is not abiding. Therefore I say that the mind of the bodhisattvas should not abide in the form of charity. Subhūti, if a bodhisattva practices charity while abiding in [notions of] the teaching, is like a person in the dark who cannot see anything. If a bodhisattva practices charity while not abiding in [notions of] the teaching, it is like a person with eyes wide open in the sunlight, seeing all kinds of forms.'

Under normal circumstances, almost everyone will conceive of their aspiration to achieve Buddhahood when they are abiding in some realm. The 'mind is abiding' when we have a mind full of attachments. Whatever the mind abides in will fetter us. The deeper we abide, the tighter the binds; the longer we abide, the stronger our binds. So, the Buddha taught that we 'should give rise to the aspiration that has no abode'. When we finally achieve this, our mind will enter a state of non-attachment, becoming a non-dualist, non-differentiating mind. This is the Buddha state, the state of non-self. In this state our mind is pure, calm, tranquil, light. It is free from suffering, affliction and fear. You could say that this state is the bodhisattva or Buddha state. It is the ultimate state for a practitioner of Dharma to attain.

An already enlightened person does not necessarily only experience good fortune and good things. In fact, they experience the whole range of possible situations, as they accept the origination gladly, whatever comes their way. They accept that what should happen, happens. Laypeople experience emotional reactions depending on what is happening in the moment and how we perceive it, whether that be good, bad, ugly or beautiful, but the enlightened person perceives all equally, without differentiation, 'To face sufferings without worry, and happiness without rejoicing' (Bodhidharma, *Treatise on Pacifying the Mind*). They experience no emotional shifts, no matter what happens to them or what situation comes to pass. They in all moments tranquil and comfortable. From this you you might realise that the difference between mundane life and awakened life lies in perspective.

The worldly perspective is that we should pursue the good and reject the bad, and that when we achieve the good, we should go after the even better. Such desirous thinking knows no bounds and inevitably leads to suffering. The enlightened person views both the good and the bad as natural phenomena, nothing more than transient manifestations in the present moment. They have a deep understanding that everything exists in a constant state of change, and that there is no need to react emotionally to such changes. Dependent origination has its natural rhythms and laws. The changes that occur following dependent arising become gradually more powerful, while the changes that occur in the run up to cessation become gradually weaker. These are unstoppable tendencies, so go with the flow and embrace the present moment. This is the way of nature and of Buddha Dharma.

Chan advocates that we embrace every natural process in life and live in the present moment. When we are hungry, we should eat; when tired, we should sleep; we should study when we must, and work when it is time. We should wholly and selflessly immerse ourselves in the present moment, in what is natural, in every detail of our life. Our mind has no fetter, and no abode. The myriad things change in accordance with causes and conditions. They are 'like a mirror, in which there is nothing but the ability to reflect all things.' Like a mirror, they only reflect the situation as it is at present. They have no expectations of what is to come, and they reflect things as they truly are; they do not cling to memories of the past and do not await the future; they abide by the causes and conditions of the present moment in every regard. They are like lotus flowers, which do not change their essence in accordance with causes and conditions; regardless the situation, they bear it in tranquillity. If they suffer, they simply persevere; when things are good, they simply carry on as normal. They are in union with the present, and they know contentedness.

If we hope to attain the realm of non-self and 'give rise to aspiration without abode', not only must we align ourselves with the collective, we must also respect and acknowledge everything that the collective gives us, like our body and appearance. Whatever we are we owe to the collective, only by realising this can we live in harmony with the natural order. If we are unsatisfied with what nature gives us, and we hope to change it through plastic surgery or tattoos, for example, then regardless of our opinion of how much more attractive we have become, we will be hurting on the inside. It is hard to imagine how damaging such a lack of respect can be.

Of course, surgery to correct a true physiological issue is fine, but that is different. Aligning with nature is the natural way of the universe; changing what nature gives us may bring fleeting happiness, but in the long term, violating the natural order in this way inevitably has a price. 'The wise allow things to change without changing themselves, thereby arising no assessment of good or bad; the ignorant strive to change themselves without considering external conditions, thereby becoming tied to considerations about whether the situation is favourable or otherwise.' Align oneself with the essential nature of the myriad things and selflessly abide by the natural order. This is how we should conduct our lives and cultivation, and Master Bodhidharma showed us the way.

All phenomena are the result of the coalescence of causes and conditions. Love and its absence, selfish and selfless love – they are all the same in this sense. In real life, for many people, love is based on the notion of an existence of selfhood. Such artificial love of anything implies the existence of things one does not love. Yet, it is humankind's innate nature to be good, and we are imbued with a benevolent love, which when we embody non-self, comes forth to shine love on all things. Seeing a child fall into a river, most people will instinctively jump in to save them. This is a natural manifestation of the non-self nature of mind, it is also a natural manifestation of selfless love. Within mundane life, love between people is hard won and hard to come by. Its essence is service and giving of oneself, it is centring your life around another person. Giving of oneself in a self-centred way is a selfish kind of love. Only love that is centred on others and is pressure-free is selfless love. That is true love.

In the world of Buddhist Dharma, compassionate empathy and true love mean very much the same, because compassion is to bring others happiness, and empathy is to suffer in the place of others. You could say that compassionate empathy is the most noble quality a Buddhist practitioner can foster; compassionate empathy never requires reciprocation. It is thus selfless. Without embodying non-self, your compassionate empathy will be polluted with elements of selfhood; it will be impure and incomplete. Only once you have aligned with your essence of non-self can you achieve true empathy.

At the relative level, the human nature of mind has two sides, the self-nature of mind which revolves around the self, and the non-self nature of mind, which is centred on the collective. The motive for human behaviour can also be divided between the self-interested and the altruistic. As laypeople, we have not yet fostered the habit of giving rise to aspiration with regard to our practice and lifestyle; experienced practitioners, especially those who cultivate Mahayana Buddhism, realise the importance of developing aspiration, which serves as their motive throughout their cultivation. When a practitioner truly develops the aspiration to help others, everything they do will come from a place of non-self.

The aspiration to help others helps stop us from acting according to the whims of the self. Otherwise, for much of our lives, we let the self take the driver's seat, which inevitably creates suffering for ourselves and for others. The more you help your self, the more likely you are to fall deeper under its influence; the more you help others, the easier it becomes to manifest non-self. At the core of giving rise to aspiration is the intent to help others, which extends to living in service of everything outside the self. It can mean helping family members, strangers or any sentient being you come across; helping society or nature. You could say that helping others aids our progress toward the complete manifestation of non-self, which is one of the most important gates in the Buddhist practice; it is a road all practitioners must travel.

Nikaya Buddhism takes transcendence of the self as its objective. It does not emphasise helping other sentient beings, it only talks about not harming them. Nikaya Buddhism also discusses maintaining a 'little self' throughout one's cultivation, which has led to some suggestions that the Nikayan path toward liberation is not absolute. By comparison, Mahayana asks a greater, more ambitious goal of its practitioners: to help liberate all other sentient beings from suffering. A Mahayanan practitioner must avoid the self, no matter what, including the 'little self'. Non-self must guide their cultivation. Developing an aspiration to live a life of non-self is the method recommended by Mahayana to help practitioners ensure their actions are not influenced by selfish intent. No matter your perspective or your thinking, as long as your actions, be they physical or mental, intend to help others in a selfless way, then you will accrue good karma; selfishness can only lead to bad karma. A Mahayana practitioner who can live wholly selflessly in service of other sentient beings has unlimited karmic merit awaiting them.

Everything is the result of the coalescence of causes and conditions. This is the origin of the myriad things, it is also the essence of the myriad things. The essence of the myriad things determines their nature. You could say that 'impermanence' and 'non-self' are the intrinsic nature of the myriad things of the universe. Upholding the right view of 'impermanence' and 'non-self' is the first step upon the journey of cultivating Dharma, aligning oneself with the intrinsic nature of the myriad things and wholly embodying non-self is the end goal of Dharmic practice.

The Buddha described his teachings as methods for gaining insight into the true form of things, but they are not themselves the true form. In a sense they are like the finger that points to the moon. The finger is still a finger, and the moon is the moon. Do not confuse the finger for the moon.

The intrinsic nature of things is like the 'moon' in the above analogy, and the wisdom of emptiness is the finger that points toward it. For us laypeople in mundane society, we are used to observing the superficial appearance of phenomena, which often leads us astray. Without the guidance of Dharmic wisdom, it is difficult for us to see to the essential nature of things; if we can foster the wisdom of emptiness, we have a chance of perceiving the true form and nature of things.

At the same time, we must bear in mind that emptiness and the wisdom of emptiness are two separate things. Emptiness is immutable. It does not change in accordance with causes and conditions. It is eternal. Wisdom of emptiness, as well as any teaching method or cultivation technique or concept, is man-made. It changes in accordance with origination. So, no teaching can be a universal principle. Buddhist teachings simply aim to guide us using wisdom based on perception of the universal principle. Seeing the 'moon' is to see the true nature of things and of the mind. Once we have achieved this, we begin to perceive the truth of the universe in everything.

The Buddha repeatedly warned practitioners not to stop their practice once they have shifted their perspective to that of Buddhist Dharma, as the next step in cultivation is even more important in our journey toward liberation. We must use our acquired knowledge and new perspective to practice observing the essential nature of the myriad things as well as to awaken to the nature of our minds. We must ask ourselves whether possessing knowledge of impermanence is enough to rid us of expectations and attachments; whether knowledge of non-self is enough to stop us acting in a selfish way. Thinking and doing are very different things, and turning an idea into action is one of the hardest things to do.

Although teachings and knowledge are not universal principles, still, attaining knowledge of 'impermanence' and 'non-self' through the Buddha's teachings can decide the quality of a person's whole life, changing its course for the better. All of the

Buddha's teachings share a single objective: to purify us of the influence of the self and manifest non-self. That goes for all 84,000 of the practices Buddhism prescribes. As long as we embody our nature of non-self, we can truly realign ourselves with the present moment, live in harmony with the collective and awaken the essential nature of the mind.

Non-self is the root of emptiness, it is the core of Buddhist Dharma, it is the essential nature of the universe—this is the absolute truth, the true form of all things.

Epilogue

Emptiness is the essential nature of the myriad things, the core of which is non-self. Non-self is the foundational nature of the myriad phenomena. It represents an absence of self, as well as an absence of expectations, attachment and suffering

Many people, myself included, have at some point misunderstood the Dharmic notion of emptiness. In fact, I remember someone telling me once that awakening to emptiness bestowed a person with a special power, like telekinesis or the ability to pass through walls or to shrink and grow the body at will. It was only later on that I realised this was a misinterpretation. Dharmic emptiness refers directly to the essential nature of the myriad things; the essential nature of the myriad things is emptiness; emptiness is the essential nature of the myriad things. Seeing to the intrinsic nature of the myriad things and aligning oneself with it - that is in and of itself a superpower.

But of course, emptiness and this special power - to understand emptiness - are two different things. One does not precede the other, since the essential nature of emptiness is immutable, eternal, it does not change in accordance with shifts in causes and conditions, and is not itself a cause nor a condition. Whereas the 'special power' is conditional, just as is any phenomenon. It is the result of origination and, therefore, reliant on the alignment of causes and conditions to exist. It is fundamentally an illusion, like a flower in a mirror or the moon's reflection in the water.

Many Buddhist texts refer to the manifestation of special abilities. I understand them as nothing more than the convenient means passed down by the Buddha by which a practitioner can bring themselves closer to enlightenment. The *Vimalakirti Sutra* explains that a bodhisattva can be wise yet lack practice in these methods; such a bodhisattva will lack compassion, even in their wisdom. This is a kind of sickness. But if a bodhisattva follows the methods laid down by the Buddha and hones their practice, they can attain liberation. A lot of the time, the special powers that manifest fit with the method practised, novice practitioners need to differentiate.

Concepts such as 'self', 'impermanence', 'relative and absolute truth' are already difficult for most people to wrap their heads around and accept. Many people do not even have a basic understanding of essential nature. In which case, it is impossible to recognise the essential nature within the myriad things - emptiness. This is why the Buddha, possessed of extraordinary wisdom, on realising that people are gifted with vastly different qualities and ways of understanding the world, and that each learns best through a specific method accordingly, designed these gates – these expedient means – through which different people are able to enter into the world of Buddhist Dharma.

It is said that he taught 84,000 methods in total, although we know that the number is only meant to indicate that there were many teachings. These methods share a common objective: to guide people toward purifying themselves of the influence of the self and selfish habits, and manifesting the essential nature of non-self. In other words, these methods aim to help us to turn our attention from the outside world and inwards, to awaken to the essential nature of the mind and attain liberation. They are the route toward awakening to the universal principle, to the essential nature of the myriad things. They help us to see through the superficial existence of phenomena to their true form and nature. Hopefully, you have realised by now that these different phrases mean much the same.

The world we live in is formed of myriad phenomena, which take various and sundry forms throughout the trajectory of their manifestations, enough to make the head spin. Frustrated, confused, overwhelmed and without connection to the true form of things, we live at the mercy of the self, and at risk of expectations and attachments leaving us battered and bruised. The myriad things all share the same essential nature, regardless their appearance; none has more or less of it, and none is purer or more defiled, or older or newer. Dharma tells us that the essential nature of the myriad things is their true form; no matter how a thing changes and evolves, its essential nature remains the same, so seeing clearly to the essential nature of one thing is equivalent to seeing to the essence of all things. Dharmic emptiness corresponds to the essential nature of the myriad things; the essential nature is emptiness; emptiness is the essential nature. A view of emptiness helps us to see to the true form of the myriad things.

The 84,000 methods were designed to guide us closer to alignment with the essential nature of all things. Among them, observing the precepts is one of the most basic methods of Buddhist practice. This has been the case since the time there were only five precepts in Buddhism's early days (do not kill, do not steal, no sexual misconduct, no lies, and no alcohol), even with the hundreds, even thousands, more precepts that have necessarily been added thereafter. In temples with strict management, monks must strictly follow and obey the precepts, at the risk of severe punishment should they break them. The precepts demand respect.

Novice practitioners of Buddhism have not yet shed the influence of the 'self'. At this stage in one's cultivation, it is important to remember that a desirous, rampant, wilful driving force such as the self likes to do whatever it wants, and so what it fears most are the precepts – discipline. For the self, the precepts represent a binding power like that of the curse put on the Monkey King with the intention of restraining his roguish character. A practitioner determined to practice the Dharma must therefore observe the precepts that will help fetter the self and protect their practice. In the process of adapting to the new lifestyle the precepts create, the practitioner will already have started on their way toward purifying their spiritual nature.

The same is true for practitioners who incorporate a meditation practice into their lives, as a means of training their concentration. At the core of Chan cultivation is the present moment. Bringing oneself into the present moment fosters a quality of selflessness; living in the present moment, free of the influence of the self, is what is known as having achieved a Chan state. The self hinders us from being present, as it tries desperately to multitask. Meditation brings us out of distraction into concentration. On a deeper level, it also exercises and improves awareness.

The mind is easily influenced by the external environment and internal, self-driven thinking. Meditation provides awareness and shows us how to settle the mind amid constant distraction. Awareness is our only tool against the self. If a practitioner has no awareness, or does not turn their awareness on the self, then they will struggle to reach their potential in their practice. For those who meditate, delusional thoughts represent the number one enemy. These result from attachment to the ego – to our notion of self. Quieting the self quietens these thoughts.

Meditation, then, is the practice of self-awareness – of fostering continuous awareness of self-attachments and delusional thinking. The day our selflessness finally, fully manifests, the self will disappear, and our delusional thoughts with it. The stronger the awareness we cultivate through meditation, the brighter the light of awareness we have to shine on the self, forcing it into retreat. In the soil of awareness, it is difficult for the self to grow; when the self-mind withers, our innate selfless nature will have the opportunity to bloom. This is why the Buddha said that the way of awareness is also the path to liberation.

In the time of the Buddha, monks would beg for food, a method for which the Buddha set the example. The beginning of the Diamond Sutra explains: 'Then, at mealtime, the World-honoured One put on his robe, took his bowl, and went into the great city of Śrāvastī to seek alms food, going from house to house within the city. Finishing, he returned home and took his meal. He then put away his robe and bowl, washed his feet, arranged his seat and sat down.' The key lesson to be taken from this passage is that the Buddha did not have preferences, he went 'from house to house within the city', skipping none and approaching all equally;

he did not have a dualistic sense of differentiation. The Buddha said that the process of begging for food is a process of letting go of the self and of arrogance and exercising humility. Whoever gives food must be treated equally, and all food should be accepted with an equal heart. It is easy to exercise humility, but it is difficult to exercise non-differentiation. Nowadays, there are still people who practice begging as a means of breaking down their arrogance and tempering their humility, but few of them consider themselves up to task of exercising that most precious of qualities – indifference. Non-duality is an important part of emptiness. Non-dualist thinking is an important prerequisite for embodying non-self. To have cultivated non-dualist thinking is to have all but completed the Dharma practice.

Besides this, Buddhism prescribes chanting, offerings, giving alms, prostrations before the Buddha, making dedications and vows and much more, as means of achieving the goal of purifying the self and revealing one's innate, selfless nature. The 84,000 gates of the Buddhist practice are meant as an expedient means to success in the practice. Different forms of practice suit different people, in different situations, at different stages of their cultivation. They can be catered to or handpicked to address specific problems, like improper thinking and selfish habits, as the moment calls for it. In other words, they require that we take into consideration the underlying causes and conditions of a situation in order to ensure we choose the appropriate method. These forms of practice are so diverse that some of them, when listed together, even seem to contradict each other in their content and intent.

Choosing a suitable practice requires wisdom. At the very least, we should avoid becoming attached to any one method, because our causes and conditions will change, and the practice will have to change accordingly. This is how we reach the ultimate goal: transcending the self, dualism, time and space, and achieving complete selflessness, the highest realm of being. According to my understanding, this is the state of Nirvana; it lies beyond all expedient means. Therefore, only with the wisdom of emptiness can we hope to match our practice methods to the current state of our individual cultivation.

Everything is the result of the combination of causes and conditions. This is the cosmic truth the Buddha awoke to beneath the bodhi tree; it is the foundation of Buddhism. Nothing can exist independently from other things. The appearance of any kind of thing may lead to the possibility of other things. All that exists in the universe is mutually dependent.

Interdependence is what makes us identify with family members, friends, classmates, colleagues, neighbours or strangers in the street; a blue sky, white clouds, mountains, forests and rivers; animals whether they are our pets or not, and plants, in our gardens or the wild; the utensils in our home or at the shop – all of these are in some way a part of our lives and we must not underestimate the importance of that fact. Cherish them and love them and you will be cherishing and loving your own life. Imbuing our view of the world with faith in universal mutual dependence helps us to cherish the people and things around us even more, making it easier to cultivate an equal and non-differentiating mode of thinking, thereby furthering us toward the goal of embodying non-self.

All things are the result of causes and conditions. The present origination is what decides the state of the universe and all it contains. Non-dualist thinking would reveal that, equally, every moment is critical in determining the quality of our life, too, and the trajectory of our life in the future. Awareness of our level of presence would tell us whether we are properly carrying out the role assigned to us within the present moment.

Of course, we have different roles and identities under different circumstances. In class, our role is to be student; at the wheel, our role is to be a driver; out for a run, our role is to be a runner; at work, a boss, a manager or an employee. Awareness helps us to fulfil that role as well as we can, without distraction. Trying to satisfy multiple roles at once and busying ourselves with multiple things inevitably pulls us away from the present, leaving us vulnerable to frustrations and anxiety. Focusing on the sole task at hand ensures that we complete it to the best of our ability, keeps us present, and makes for a calmer, less stressful day.

Since everything is the result of causes and conditions, no phenomenon in the universe is permanent.

In order to break from any attachment to the existence of 'constancy' or 'permanence', the Buddha expounded the concepts of 'existence' and 'appearance' or 'manifestation'. Obviously, if we see all things as having 'existence', we leave ourselves open to falling into the vicious cycle of expectation and attachment, because we wrongly believe that things will not change – that things always exist, that good things are always good, and that bad things are always bad.

As with the delusional belief that there is such thing as a 'self', the more strongly we convince ourselves that there exists 'permanence' in the universe, the deeper our attachments will become, and the more we will suffer when our expectations are foiled. If, instead, we look at the world as a tapestry of 'appearances' – nothing more than transient and illusory 'manifestations' – our perspective on the world and the situations we find ourselves in will become much more flexible, because we are prepared for change. This kind of thinking is itself an aspect of the wisdom of emptiness.

We have all experienced something we expected to go well taking a turn for the worse, or something we had dismissed as a failure giving us a pleasant surprise. This is part of this journey toward understanding the futility of our expectations and the lack of permanence in the universe, to embracing the essence of things, the essence of life and impermanence.

We all need to learn to accept impermanence. It is immanent in everything – not only the external environment and phenomena, but in ourselves too. It is vital that we make sufficient psychological preparation to face impermanence in all aspects of

148

life. This is the key to shifting our our perspective and transforming negative emotions into positive energy, turning our troubles into Bodhi.

It is also vital that we discover the Buddha nature within ourselves. In doing so, we will unlock our true selves. We will live in the present at all times. We will intuitively know what we should do and what we should not do; we will receive the guidance of our inner voice when it comes to choosing a career and hobbies. Do not underestimate this inner voice, because it is the manifestation of our true nature. We will find ourselves more engaged and focused in everything we do and our non-self will shine forth.

The longer we can remain in this state, the easier it will become. Our lives will make us ever more serene and contented; that is the magic of unlocking the true self. Remember that, as I explained at the end of Chapter 4, the true self is a relative concept used only to help us laypeople to understand the stages of the practice. Realising one's nature and regaining the true self are only the first goals of practice. Embodying our inner non-self is the ultimate goal. Only then is it possible to live in acceptance of the inherent nature of all things, follow the natural path of the universe, and shed any and all suffering.

The sea of suffering is boundless. Whenever and wherever the self is allowed to flourish, mental disorders, insomnia, depression, irritability, family discord, emotional chaos, professional frustrations and lifelessness abound. The more self-centred a person, the more prone they are to suffering. This is the truth to which the Buddha hoped to awaken all sentient beings. The major psychological schools and mental health treatment methods of the modern world are based on helping to free patients from their suffering. If any of these philosophies and practices helps patients to realise that at the core of their sickness lies the corrupting self, then it has a chance of success. If any of them can also show patients they possess a powerful sense of non-self within themselves, then it stands as the best there is.

It is a pity, then, that certain psychological treatments fail to correctly identify and communicate the source of patients' suffering, never giving them the knowledge and the tools to truly break themselves out of the cycle of suffering. Even the merest nudge in the right direction, toward realising that the source of their suffering is the self, is preferable.

I often used to hear people say that the karmic rewards gained by studying Buddhism are great, but I didn't yet know this for myself. Now I look back on those times and sigh in admiration at the insight of those people. They were right. And so were the first Buddhists. Dharma comprises a body of wisdom and collection of practices guided by a truth that penetrates the surface of phenomena to their core, directing us to the essential nature within. Studying and practicing Buddhism not only increases our wisdom, but also removes bad life habits. It shows us that the universe is imbued with impermanence and selflessness. When we realise this we begin the next stage of our lives, leading an ever less selfish, anxiety-ridden and painful existence. It can thus be our saviour.

Everything results from the coalescence of causes and conditions. The whole of the world around us – mountains, rivers, ground, birds and beasts; airplanes, guns, computers and mobile phones – all derives from the original material of the universe, which itself took shape from some material that preceded it. Since then, matter has changed state and shifted form in accordance with causes and conditions; this is the unchanging destiny of the universe. It will see no end. The old ceases to be, and the new takes its place. Life and death are big deals for humans, but they are nothing to the universe. They simply represent the transformation of one kind of matter into another. There is never any increase or decrease in the mount of matter in the universe. This is Buddhism's wisdom of emptiness.

The intrinsic nature of all things is emptiness, and the core of emptiness is non-self.

Non-self is the foundation and nature of all phenomena. Non-self signifies an absence of self, as well as an absence of expectation, attachment and suffering. The myriad things abide by the way of nature and the shifting causes and conditions that underlie it. All manifestations of self run counter to the essential nature of non-self, and all expectations and attachments are contrary to nature. The previous chapters have explained that on a secular, relative level, the self-nature of mind is innate to humans. When our self is operating, expectations and attachments will arise with the self. A certain degree of selfhood, of expectation and attachment, is acceptable, even necessary at times, but unfettered selfhood devoid of awareness can easily get out of control, at which time everything becomes discordant and unsatisfactory, and suffering quickly follows.

We create so much suffering for ourselves, yet we often forget where our suffering comes from – selfishness and self-centredness and an incorrect view of life and our place within the world. It is a perspective rife with confusion, as it sometimes brings us brief happiness, but more often, as we will realise through awareness, only worsens our suffering. Unfortunately, without wisdom it is almost impossible for us to perceive the essence of our suffering and misconceptions.

Selfish habits left unchecked for years on end become ingrained. So much so that no ordinary psychological treatments or mundane thinking can shake their foundation. Wisdom alone has the power to bring the self under control again. Wisdom is the best medicine for curing emotional suffering.

Buddhist Dharma takes emptiness as its guiding principle. At its core is non-self. It views complete selflessness as the highest possible realm to be achieved through cultivation. Non-self is the root of all phenomena; it is their nature. A mind of non-self is a pure mind; it is the only thing able to save all sentient beings from suffering.

Hearing and thinking only produce knowledge. We must use our body to experience, realise and embody our learning in order to gain insights that we can put to changing our lives. Experience and wisdom accumulated over time in this way are valuable beyond any amount of material wealth. Truth and wisdom are priceless.

Printed in Great Britain
by Amazon

17453011R00092